'Lily Dunn is one of our best teachers and theorists of autobiographical writing and *Into being* is an inspiring, philosophical and helpful guide. If you are a memoirist feeling discouraged or lost, this book will give you both encouragement and insight into the value of the form, and practical ways forward. I copied many lines into my own journal.'

Amy Liptrot, author of *The Instant*

'As astute as it is generous, Lily Dunn's *Into being* draws a capacious doorway for all who seek to write from lived experience, illuminating the contours of the endeavour using copious examples and abundant wisdom.'

Melissa Febos, author of *The Dry Year*

'A beautiful book: absorbing, propulsive, generous and humane, both in its honesty and in its willingness to share process.'

Marina Benjamin, author of *A Little Give*

'*Into being* is a startlingly beautiful book that unpacks the craft of memoir with compassion and vast wisdom. Lily Dunn has written an indispensable companion for any writer embarking on the time-bending, often overwhelming journey that is the creation of memoir. I loved everything about it, and I'll be giving copies to all of my students.'

Elissa Altman, author of *Permission: The New Memoirist and the Courage to Create*

'A profound examination of the value of memoir for both writer and reader, with practical advice on how to access emotionally meaningful events. Lily Dunn's *Into being* is the essential guide to all things memoir.'

Richard Beard, author of *The Day That Went Missing*

'*Into being* could not be more timely. Life writing, memoir and autobiographical storytelling are culturally prevalent and Lily Dunn has provided us with a sensitively written, wise and insightful combination of advice, reflection and theory. An instant classic that I will be using in my teaching and writing life.'

Suzanne Joinson, author of *The Museum of Lost and Fragile Things*

'A revelatory and vibrant exploration of the transformative power of memoir – an essential read for writers, readers and teachers.'

Jenn Ashworth, author of *The Parallel Path*

'This book is a gift to the serious memoirist or life writer looking to develop their work. Full of practical advice, inspiring examples and a generous breadth of references, *Into being* looks set to become an essential part of any writer's toolkit.'

Julia Bell, author of *Hymnal*

Into being

Manchester University Press

Into being

The radical craft of memoir and its power to transform

Lily Dunn

MANCHESTER UNIVERSITY PRESS

Copyright © Lily Dunn 2025

The right of Lily Dunn to be identified as the author of this work has been asserted in accordance with the Copyright, Designs and Patents Act 1988.

Published by Manchester University Press
Oxford Road, Manchester, M13 9PL

www.manchesteruniversitypress.co.uk

British Library Cataloguing-in-Publication Data
A catalogue record for this book is available from the British Library

ISBN   978 1 5261 7925 8   hardback

First published 2025

The publisher has no responsibility for the persistence or accuracy of URLs for any external or third-party internet websites referred to in this book, and does not guarantee that any content on such websites is, or will remain, accurate or appropriate.

EU authorised representative for GPSR:
Easy Access System Europe, Mustamäe tee 50, 10621 Tallinn, Estonia
gpsr.requests@easproject.com

Typeset
by New Best-set Typesetters Ltd

For Robin, with love

Contents

Preface

You might have picked up this book because you are interested in writing memoir for publication, or because you write for therapeutic purposes, for your own well-being – or maybe you are interested in both. Maybe you picked it up because you love *reading* memoir and want to know more about how a memoir is created, from idea through to publication. Or maybe you are just intrigued by the title. This book is a craft book to a certain degree, but not in an obvious sense. It is not a how-to book, that follows a formula, because in my view the process of writing memoir is too personal and organic in its growth for that. It could never throw its net so wide. It is also not a book about writing for well-being. If there is a therapeutic outcome, it happens accidentally, as a sweet addition to crafting a beautiful piece of writing, something artful, to share with others. You will find me addressing the tricky nature of memory here, of course, and memory's relationship with the imagination and ways to explore this through speculative forms of writing, because all writing – however much it is rooted in real-life experience – is creation.

This book follows the process of bringing a memoir into being. I use my own experience, where illuminating, of writing and publishing my memoir, *Sins of My Father: A Daughter, a Cult, a Wild Unravelling*, and my years of teaching and mentoring personal narrative. I am particularly interested in the dance between writing and gaining in self-understanding in life, and how intimately connected they are. I have always leaned on writing to help me through major transformative decisions in my personal life, and my personal experience has always influenced my writing. I can only speak for myself, but in doing so I also attempt to show you how to speak for yourselves.

By sharing my knowledge, I hope to empower those who are interested in memoir to feel more confident to write it. I am a teacher and mentor, as much as a writer, not simply because teaching is how I earn my living, but because I happen to love it. Teaching memoir transcends the wildest of dreams of a young girl who knew from an early age that she wanted to be a writer, and instinctively wrote from life, even in her fiction. I discovered writing out of necessity: I learned early its power to make me feel better, simply by transmutation from head or heart, to gut, then arm, to pen, to words on a page. And that those words were in my command: I could bring life to difficult experience, find meaning in pain, make it beautiful by turning it into story, and if it wasn't working, I could simply start again. I learned early that doing this made life more bearable.

This was my first lesson in personal empowerment. It gives me immense pleasure to share this power with others to help them overcome their fear of how writing personal narrative might be considered indulgent, or solipsistic

– look at me! – or might hurt those they love, because I know how much writing has helped me understand, then transcend, the more challenging aspects of my own self. I could read and write about memoir for the rest of my life, and I would be happy. I love its intimate nature, and the way it connects lives, its frankness and dedication to honesty; the satisfaction in the small voice at the back of my mind that tells me while reading – *this is a true story!*

What is a memoir, exactly? It is a difficult term to define, which is perhaps why it is easier to emphasise what a memoir *isn't*, rather than what it *is*. A memoir is not autobiography, which is the story of an entire life. Instead, it often examines a significant event, or series of events, for deeper and universal meaning. A memoir is not fiction, and a memoir is not a novel, but it does often use novelistic techniques. While a memoir can be about someone other than the author, as is the case with my own memoir, *Sins of My Father*, it is not biography, because what is described is only what is experienced by the author, who is also the book's narrator, seen through the prism of their subjective understanding. A memoir is as much a form of literary art – with use of speculative and enhanced detail – as it is an attempt to touch on the truth of the lived experience from which it originates.

Reality and truth are of course slippery notions, but memoir has a commitment to dig deep into its subject, 'to lay bare the questions that have been hidden by the answers', as James Baldwin wrote, to touch the nerve of personal truth, however complex and shifting that might be – or at the very least, it has a willingness to try. Memoir does not pretend to know the answers, just as we can never really pin our life like a butterfly on a board, but it attempts to ask the right questions. And it is the bridge between personal narrative and a lived life that I find most fascinating. When teaching or mentoring writers, one-to-one, it often feels as if we are touching on questions not only of how to write better, but also how to live better, to be more self-aware and honest as we move through the world. The best memoirs, I believe, evolve alongside their authors who gain in understanding and wisdom the longer they live with their material. In the end, the story and the life become symbiotic.

I don't think I am being too idealistic to say that what might accompany this new understanding is not only a fresh way of looking at ourselves, but also renewed relationships with those we love and those who are affected by the story. This is part of memoir's therapeutic power. But its effects can be both good and bad, depending on whether family members or loved ones see the world through the same prism, or have a preparedness to try, or whether they find it an imposition and an invasion of their own privacy. Either way, one of the more challenging aspects of writing memoir, and one of the reasons many writers just don't go there, is that it often pushes relationships with loved ones into new territory.

My argument is not that writing memoir is therapeutic (although it can barely escape such deep challenges and changes), but more that the process can bring about transformation. You set out to write a particular experience, something that happened in your life, and by doing so you hold it to the light and begin to see it differently. You talk to other family members, you look more closely at letters or photographs, read books related to the subject, gain in deeper understanding, and your perspective changes again. Because you change, the story changes: the story changes and you change too; a living presence on the page. At some point you reach the end, and an editor gives their input, and the book is published, and it has a life of its own. But that life continues without you, transformed by its readers into part of their story, and through reviews and feedback this alters you and your relationship with your own most personal experience.

Without necessarily meaning to, a writer of memoir finds themselves moving through the world slightly differently. If we can embrace the pain of facing difficult experience and challenge our old way of thinking about our lives, we gain in greater insight and understanding. Exposure lifts the veil on the unspoken, the unthought even, so it can be faced, and what follows should be renewal, of some kind, even if the road has at times appeared impassable. By writing memoir, we are committed to the long haul, and I am reassured that even when it feels as if the world is against you, transformation is possible. Writing memoir has the potential to rescue you from the insidiousness of unprocessed experience, and help make you into a more complete human being.

As part of my research for this book, I had conversations with other memoirists about their own process, both published and working towards publication. You'll find their voices adding piquancy throughout, and their answers to select questions at the end. Speaking with others also feels fitting in a book about the relationship we have with ourselves, those we write about and the world (including our readers).

The voices that appear in the book belong to insightful and courageous writers: Pragya Agarwal, Jade Angeles

Fitton, Jenn Ashworth, Polly Atkin, Damian Barr, Richard Beard, Julia Bell, Marina Benjamin, Clare Best, Susanna Crossman, Caro Giles, Lorelei Goulding, Dr Tulika Jha, Tom Lee, Noreen Masud, Leah McLaren, Ali Millar, Mary J. Oliver, Vanessa Springora, Clover Stroud, Catherine Taylor, Kit de Waal and Anna Wilson.

By looking more closely at the discoveries I have made as a reader of memoir, a writer and then through the experience of being published, I hope to give other memoirists, both new and established, a model to use or adapt in navigating their own, often fascinating, sometimes hazardous, writing journey. It is a personal adventure in process, with tips and exercises that should help anyone interested in writing or teaching memoir. A tool, but also, I hope, a helping hand.

As someone who at times feels such an impulse to write and will write on whatever is to hand, whether on a napkin or the back of an envelope, to me it feels fitting to include images of some of these at the start of each chapter. Also, as part of my writing practice, I keep a notebook of inspirational quotes about writing personal narrative, and so it feels natural to also reference the writers who have influenced my work. One of my favourites is by Patricia Hampl: 'No one owns the past, but it is a grave error (another age would have said a grave sin) not to inhabit memory. Sometimes I think it is all we really have.'

he mother was ill used. May had Stella
Picture gave at   2 v Renoirs 4 —
corfu - advance   2 - 5 - one no south
was out.   in dress. Corfu —
£500 advance   — 2 v 4 in corfu.
Some home are   out - 78. Teddy with
with Teddy   upside down
yo2 —
D-d would cycle   back from
             Doble   in the Kentgloba Church
Street, In the   Spres. But you.
May would their   Nee i Mun beigh head
duty and Red home.   She had yay chide
d was into Nepenthe   & constantly give I'm
what he   childre die. The
the 6-w Teddy   week tour Knelly a
foot - then Switzerland. Post N·yosterri was
was carried areas. hippie if no time

Introduction
From repatterning to becoming

'I see the scene again and again,' writes Laura Cumming at the start of her book *On Chapel Sands*, in which she attempts to reveal the hidden truth behind a mysterious kidnapping, 'trying to grasp the unfathomable moment in which she vanished and everything changed'. The kidnapping was of her mother, aged just three. Cumming writes of the pernicious power of this event, how it changed her mother, influenced her relationship with her children and 'has run through my days ever since I first heard of the incident 30 years ago'.

Much memoir and personal narrative begins with a burning question, the tug of a hand, an ache in the heart, a clutch of joy, something unresolved from the past bubbling up (or crashing) into the present. 'I've felt possessed by my past – swept up by it,' author and academic Noreen Masud tells me, 'all my life, even as it was happening.' These ghosts might slip in, disguised, through the back door of an author's fiction – a surrogate character with a changed gender, perhaps, or one who dies of disease rather than drowning – until they're not able to sidestep it any longer. Embarking on a memoir enables a writer to look closer, to go deeper, to upturn family myths and to finally gain insight into what might previously have been impossible. When Laura Cumming discovers an absence, a period of years missing in a photo album of her mother's childhood, she begins to ask: why? In doing so, she helps her mother better understand her past, but also breaks an entire community's iron silence.

It takes courage and patience to write our experience in non-fiction: courage to face the past, and patience to sit with difficult experience for longer than perhaps we want to, or, more likely, than our family wants us to. Writing memoir, much like attending therapy, often probes the unspeakable, even the unthinkable, to give it voice, and to find meaning; and crafting a memoir gives shape to the chaos of everyday suffering and of joy. It also involves what the essayist and memoirist Vivian Gornick names a process of 'becoming': the movement in the narrative – the story's momentum and drive – advances with the 'I' of the narrator's evolution into a more integrated human being; from someone caught in the surf, thrown this way and that, a victim to circumstance and the rush of the tide, to someone standing despite the sharp stones and shifting pebbles beneath their feet, able to walk steadily to the shore. This self-realisation in the narrator should also offer greater clarity in the author's own life. Describing writing and publishing *A Flat Place*, Masud tells me: 'giving my life a finished form, making it into a paper object distinct from myself – rather than something shapeless which suffuses my whole body and interrupts me when I try to speak, with a voice only I can hear – has been an extraordinary relief'. Writing (and publishing) memoir then becomes an act of radical liberation for ourselves, and, as we'll touch on throughout this introduction, for our readers. What if the memoir becomes a kind of 'third space', a constellation of memories and archive from the past, given shape by a burgeoning understanding in the present: felt emotion, image, letters, journals and books read, conversations had, lessons learned, brought together by the act of writing, and all the surprises and revelations that writing itself brings? Referring to his memoir, *The Day That Went Missing*, the author Richard Beard compares writing memoir to a narrative painting: 'In a memoir there is a dramatic event, and then in real life there is the question, "and?" What happened before, what happened afterwards? I had a moment, a memory of a drowning, when I was in the water with my brother, and I asked: How did we get here?' Laura Cumming, by discovering the gaps in her family photo album, asks questions of the images that she does see. Who took the photographs? Why was her mother so often not with her parents? By looking closer she begins to understand her mother's childhood differently. What we read then is what is discovered in a writer's attempts to answer that question: the revelations, but also conversations, between multiple viewpoints on the page – with family members perhaps, but also the innocent feeling child in the immediate heat of experience, and the adult who is trying to make sense of it all. Style and technique draw the evidence together, and the craft of writing makes it whole and artful: a memoir transforms experience into story, and takes on a life of its own.

It's not an easy task: the memoirist needs to learn to be present in the vibrancy of experience – what Mary Karr calls 'feeling oneself alive in the past' – whilst simultaneously standing apart from it to see it in the round, to engage with both the participatory self and the wisdom and insight of the narrator and who they have become. In effect, a memoirist is both the analysand and the analyst: able to viscerally feel events as if they were happening again in their living room, while imparting hard-won understanding, from their reflection on these events, and their ongoing quest for survival. This demands an honesty with the self, and a clarity that only comes with confidence and distance. The clinical psychologist Arabella Kurtz describes something similar when talking about the role of psychotherapy, in conversation with J. M. Coetzee, in *The Good Story*: 'The two processes, the patient pouring out what is inside them and therapist and patient working together to give outpourings a form and meaning which is broadly sympathetic but also involves facing up to complex and painful truths, are interdepend-ent.' The 'evacuation' as she describes it, is only part of the process. While writing, the memoirist does something similar: the narrator uses their hard-won wisdom to make sense of past experience.

There is the well-worn antagonism, artificially erected by critics of the idea of the therapeutic element in writing: that writing for well-being and 'writing well' are on oppos-ing sides of a debate about literary quality. In one, the emphasis is on self-expression and not on the end product – the initial 'writing out' or 'evacuation' (using Kurtz's word) given precedence over rewriting and structuring – whereas the concept of 'writing well' is often applied to a writer aiming for publication with more emphasis on storytelling technique and artfulness over process. What if memoir complicates this? It is both the 'process' and the 'technique' that can result in transformation and healing.

Many memoirs start their life in a journal or a diary, like Anna Wilson's memoir, *A Place for Everything*, about her mother's late diagnosis of autism, which started as 'a messy, raw outpouring of anger at the situation my parents and I found ourselves in … During the most acute times I did what I have always done and scribbled it down, unedited and un-crafted, for no one's eyes but my own.' But, by starting a blog and inviting readers – albeit at that time only friends and family – Wilson took her first step away from the 'raw outpouring' of her diary-writing. When one particular friend pleaded with Wilson to turn her blog into a book, 'I had no choice but to wrestle my unwieldly blog posts and journals into a narrative arc.' The crafting began: 'Where on earth do you start when telling the story of a life?' she asked herself. 'With backstory? With scene setting? With a date of birth and from there onwards? I tried all these and they fell very flat.' Wilson then landed on a day when she felt the most unhinged – in the midst of having to care for her parents (her father was dying from cancer and her mother's mental illness was spiralling), and doing something as mundane as a supermarket shop. This and the emotion contained in it, became the book's beginning, an 'inciting incident' as it is called when teaching screenwriting and fiction.

A literary memoir, with audience in mind, is born from this secondary transmutation, from raw experience, to language, to image, to story. A writer will have gained an awareness of the difference between 'raw experience' as it is lived, and 'story' as it is told (with pacing and dramatic tension, ebb and flow); 'words' which might fall on to the page – an outpouring of feeling – and 'language', those same words or similar crafted to amplify mood, tone, emotion and character. This often involves a combination of purging and scene-setting, research and reflection, redrafting and editing, moving through varying degrees of separation from initial painful experience to polished manuscript. And it can take years. A writer needs to sit with the difficult stuff, be prepared to take risks, and jump into the unknown. They need to move through the underworld to emerge (slightly altered) on the other side.

Over time an author begins to have control over their narrative, which results in what Gornick describes in her slim and fierce book *The Situation and the Story* as a 'single piece of awareness that clarifies only slowly in the writer, gaining strength and definition as the narrative progresses'. Story is the memoir's inner dynamic, its emotional meaning and reason for being. It is, as Gornick states, 'the emotional experience that preoccupies the writer: the insight, the wisdom, the thing one has come to say'. In most cases, story is discovered through the writing itself.

While many memoirs are powerful acts of testimony, they don't simply chronicle events: this happened and then this, which resulted in this. Memoirists are as much storytellers as novelists, concerned with character, form, style and structure; this means deselecting material too – leaving a lot out. A memoir can be (well-)written any which way: its architecture might be chronological with conventional chapters, or braided with two or more timelines; it might be told backwards or in aftermath; or it might take a more poetic approach, pieced together fragments or vignettes. A memoir might be polemic and have a strong non-fiction component or it might be purely visceral.

Richard Beard's memoir is both expressive and beautifully crafted, written with the skill of a fiction writer (he wrote and published six novels before *The Day That Went Missing*), immediate and sensory, but also full of emotional honesty, particularly when capturing the complexity of denial. 'The two of us are in the sea, jumping as the waves roll in. Until now I have tried not to know this and many times I've stopped, squeezed shut my eyes and closed the memory down. I can do that, crush it out of existence. All it costs me is the effort.' The book follows Beard's attempt to grasp at the truth, collecting his evidence, so he can finally shake off his family's denial and return to the beach where his younger brother drowned forty years before. In discussion with me about this experience, Beard spoke of how important the act of writing was for him: 'I don't think I would have done it without the motivation of the writing ... If I hadn't set off on this project as a writer, I wouldn't have reached the same conclusions as a human being and lived the changes that came about because of that.' A finished memoir then becomes a manifestation of this evolution of the self, and a gift to its reader who bears witness to the intimate journey of change, revelation and sometimes even recovery.

Writing is a kind of alchemy that can release a writer from the straitjacket of how they have perceived themselves, locked into societal expectations or pressures, the right spouse, the right job, the right house on the right street. As a memoir writer and mentor, I like to help tease out what the critic and essayist Phillip Lopate calls in his instructive book on narrative non-fiction, *To*

Show and to Tell, the 'underlying shapes of experience'. When a writer begins to explore their memories, meaning reveals itself, which in turn illuminates the significance of further memories that might have seemed to be just a series of random events, fragmented and unrelated. As I'll demonstrate throughout this book, the act of writing and research unearths shape. It is a shape that is not entirely subjective, what Carl Jung calls the 'infinite' or the 'essential', that which is invisible but deeply felt if we allow ourselves to recognise it. It is shape that waits 'patiently to be brought to the surface', as Lopate argues, through the writing itself.

There are moments from our everyday experience that cling to us, asking to be better understood; or perhaps as writers we are like sculptors, slowly chiselling away the matter to touch on the infinite shape 'the eternal laws of nature and of the harmony of the spheres' as Barbara Hepworth so wisely puts it. The form finds itself, it speaks, and connects to the wider world.

But, as Masud points out, shape is not always cohesive: 'Sometimes memories can be fundamentally incompatible, they contradict each other, they're impossible, big parts are missing – and that's normal.' Writing can help us tap into an innate sense of wisdom about our own lives, and part of that wisdom is admitting to what is unknowable and unresolvable. Masud helps clarify: 'Joining the unjoinable, in a way which doesn't conceal the impossibility, which makes the impossibility part of it.' Sometimes we cannot find the answers and we cannot forgive, but memoir allows us to attempt to try.

On Chapel Sands begins with the scene that has haunted Cumming for decades: the inciting incident of her mother's kidnapping, pieced together through a daughter's knowledge of place and character, her research, analysis of photographs, through hearsay, because it happened before Cumming was born:

> This is how it began, and how it would end, on the long pale strand of a Lincolnshire beach in the last hour of sun, the daylight moon small as a kite in the sky. Far below, a child of three was playing by herself with a new tin spade. It was still strangely warm in that autumn of 1929, and she had taken off her plimsoles to feel the day's heat lingering in the sand beneath her feet.

We as readers know immediately that we are in the hands of an expert storyteller: 'I picture each scene, as we do with puzzles, assembling the evidence in the mind's eye. But the habit is involuntary.' As the daughter of two artists, Cumming has artistic sensibility, and can read pictures as well as she can paint them in prose. But *On Chapel Sands* is also as suspenseful as the best detective novels, as Cumming seeds uncertainties from the start, those facts that don't quite add up: her grandmother's slow response to the kidnapping there on the beach, 'a prolonged moment of parental inattention', and how 'everything stands in view' – there is nowhere for an adult and child to hide. As a child looking at the family photo album, Cumming never noticed the absence of photographs, which she does as an adult. There is nothing there from before the kidnapping when her mother was aged three to after she was 13.

Slowly, from close inspection of these photographs, and through conversations with her mother and members of the community, from revisiting the beach and local area, and reading her mother's own memoir, Cumming rewrites the past. Because this is essentially a memoir about her mother, it feels important to include her words, and Cumming lifts extracts from her mother's 'birthday memoir', a memoir which Cumming had insisted her mother write for her year on year to better understand what her mother considers her 'insignificant' life. With all this evidence, Cumming reveals the truth of who took her mother ('presumed stolen') that day on the beach and begins to understand her family differently. She has the compassion of a daughter, but also the dispassionate view of the narrator at one remove, who must see beyond decades of hurt to complete the picture. *On Chapel Sands* then becomes a gift to her mother of the love her mother didn't feel growing up.

What I find most interesting is the way Cumming looks to famous paintings and their details for clues – the reservation of the father in Degas's 'Family Portrait' for instance – and applies these 'universal' clues to the specifics of her family. By doing this she comments not only on universal family dynamics, but also each painter and their intentions, pointing to what is revealed and what is hidden. She calls 'Family Portrait' a psychological masterpiece: a novel in paint. 'Paintings, unlike books, don't divide between fiction and non-fiction. But this one tells a story that invites interpretation.'

On Chapel Sands in many ways is also a psychological masterpiece. Cumming has been haunted by the secrets in her past, but they have also formed her and the way she views the world. They have given her that same skill of interpretation, the ability to look beneath the surface at the beating heart within, that which refused to be subsumed by the more palatable, socially acceptable narrative. This skill transforms the family story, and also gives her memoir its transformative power. 'The photograph has not altered since I first saw it with the eyes of a child,' Cumming writes, 'but my understanding of it has changed, just like the Chapel stories my mother used to tell; I see it all anew.'

I have always associated writing with relief and transformation. When I was growing up, both my parents were writers, and I discovered writing before I discovered reading, as a means of personal expression. I was about ten when my dad gave me my first diary – it was Hello Kitty and pink – and told me to write down all that was troubling me. At the time it was mostly a deep sadness when I was around him and the young woman he had fallen in love with, who was only eight years older than me (she was 18 and at university when they met). But as I grew up, my collection of notebooks and journals grew alongside me and soon there were very few photographs of me without a notebook and pen in hand. I continued writing a diary throughout my childhood and adolescence, but I wrote stories too, which morphed into novels, which by popular demand I read in instalments to my friends at school. I began to rely on my writing a little like food; a life-giving source of nourishment and sustenance – How could I thrive without it?

There was an element of escapism to it – I would hide in the school library at breaktime, feverishly returning to the worlds I had created in whatever story I was nurturing at the time, as perhaps it was easier than negotiating friendships, other people's expectations; but I also turned to writing to work out my emotions. I have kept almost every scrap of paper I ever wrote on – which is testament to how much this process means to me.

Later, as a young woman venturing into my first relationships, falling into and out of love, I would write my feelings – particularly the confused ones – on napkins, the inside of book covers, pages torn out of sketchbooks. They were often fraught feelings, spiky and unprocessed: *I feel dread; my stomach starts to hurt and I begin to cry; the thoughts go round and round my head with this sickening feeling that everything is not okay. It's not going to be okay. What is wrong with me?? He irritates me but I love him and I don't know what I think. It's mad! I hate it!*

I instinctively entered a dialogue with myself: one voice would attack the page with a black pen and expletives, moving from anger to pain, to self-doubt and back to anger again, and then a different part of myself would assert itself, this one calmer and reassuring. *You're okay, you're okay. Everything is going to be okay.* That voice would write all the reasons why I didn't need to believe what I was telling myself: *It's in you. It's not real. You're scared that's all. You are frightened he's going to leave you, like Dad did.* It soothed my vulnerable self. This was my more rational voice, one that was growing in insight and wisdom, one that had compassion, also. Over time I learned to cultivate a relationship between the different parts of myself and became better at easing the panic and pain; each time I would return to equilibrium a little more quickly. This was a very private practice that I used as a form of personal therapy for decades, a form of survival.

These feelings later found their way into the personal essays I wrote, and my memoir, *Sins of My Father*, which pivots around my father's sudden flight from us when I was six years old, to join a cult. He disappeared without saying where he was going or for how long, and returned six months later, thin from dysentery, and dressed in the colours of the sunrise. On Hampstead High Street he told my brother and me that he had been reborn and was no longer our father. Writing my feelings down and creating shape from experience, finding my story, helped dispel those feelings. Didn't Virginia Woolf write something similar in her memoirs, *Moments of Being*? 'It is only by putting it into words that I make it whole; this wholeness means that it has lost its power to hurt me; it gives me, perhaps because by doing so I take away the pain, a great delight to put the severed parts together. Perhaps this is the strongest pleasure known to me.' And it was a pleasure and an essential life lesson to know I could help myself in such a simple (and inexpensive) way.

When my PhD supervisor, Julia Bell, encouraged me to write the non-fiction account of my father's life and my relationship with him, I resisted. I had written about him already in my first novel, *Shadowing the Sun*, so why would I go back there again? On one hand, I no longer wanted to honour him with my attention (which was short-sighted because he kept popping up into my fiction), but I also worried that writing from life was unimaginative – simply working with what was already there – and perceived by many as navel-gazing or solipsistic. Then again, I was also suffering at the time, going through a marriage separation which I was beginning to realise was in part an emotional response to unprocessed grief around my father's premature death due to alcoholism. I began impulsively writing out the pain, returning to certain memories that had haunted me for years. One such experience was the last week I saw my father, when my brother and I flew to California to try to persuade him into rehab and were confronted by a monster, a ghost of himself, hijacked by an illness we had had no idea had got such a grip on him. When this essay was taken up by *Granta* and then selected by Memoir Monday (a weekly curation of the best personal essays found on the web), I followed the scent and let the writing lead the way. My supervisor was right: there was something here that I needed to explore.

Years later, a divorce behind me and following a relocation to a new city, I had a finished book. I landed a new agent and the best editor I could have hoped for. Both my supervisor and my editor's feedback on my memoir opened my eyes to the hard psychological work of mentoring writers of personal narrative. This was as much about perception, sensitivity and boldness to probe the author and the material of her life as understanding the market. On my editor's reading of my finished draft, she felt that even though I had written my father's life in my attempt to have agency over my own, I was still trapped in a state of subservience to a man who I continued to treat as a hero despite his shocking neglect and betrayal. If I stuck with this narrative, she feared, my readers would feel let down. But I was so bound by this dynamic that had been cultivated and nurtured by him over my entire life as a way of reassuring himself of his narcissistic and fragile power, it felt like a huge psychic shift to let it go. My editor was sensitive to this, and when she talked it through with me, it suddenly became clear: Why had I not seen this before? When I was finally able to see my father clearly, I did not have to be his puppet any more. I was ready to write my final draft. In *Sins of My Father* I finally rose above as I laid his ghost to rest. A new version of our relationship had come into being. And because I had discovered a deeper truth, one that I had been blind to, I was able to have a more honest dialogue with my reader. Feedback from readers proved my editor right.

Being alert and willing to listen to those persistent memories and how they wake up the sleeping parts of our consciousness is the first step to writing memoir. But to draw them into a highly personal narrative is the satisfying part, because by doing this a writer is also beginning to orchestrate something new. I was drawn to non-fiction, because my father's compulsive lies mean I cannot stand deceit, and I look for honesty before any other human trait. The real challenge of memoir, I have realised, is sitting with experience long enough, and going deep enough to find the universals in the particular, and the beauty in the everyday. I also value how writing my memoir about my father gave me the opportunity to know him better (it was easier, perhaps, to know him in death). The more discoveries I made about his childhood at boarding school and his philandering as a young man, the more the real story started to evolve. I began to understand why this man who had everything (beauty, wealth, love) squandered it all, destroying himself and damaging everyone who loved him. In fact, the discoveries became woven into the texture of the story, which also became about me as a writer facing new versions of myself; much in the way discovering the truth behind the mysterious disappearance of Laura Cumming's mother became the driving force in *On Chapel Sands*; or finding the facts with evidence through the layers of denial becomes Richard Beard's motivation in *The Day That Went Missing*.

All good literature transcends the original idea or experience from which it was seeded. But in memoir something else is at work: the plot is less about cause and effect and more about the adventure the writer has gone on in their attempt to answer a series of questions. The journey in the end might be about redemption, but not simply personal absolution; it is more that in the process of writing and fashioning how best to express our experiences so that they resonate with others, we become more acquainted with ourselves; and the more acquainted we are with ourselves the more we can empathetically engage with others. In knowing and coming to accept the different sides of ourselves, both light and shadow, and drawing them together to make a new and more complex whole – what Carl Jung called individuation, 'bright and dark and yet neither' – we return to the words of Woolf: 'this wholeness means that it has lost its power to hurt me'. It is this that draws me back to memoir again and again: that it can make a difference to lives, not just to that of the narrator, but those the narrator writes about, their loved ones invited into the process, and even more importantly the lives of their readers. By inhabiting the lives of real people writing about real-life experience, readers of memoir can better understand their own way of living. As Lord Byron famously wrote: 'a small drop of ink ... which makes thousands, perhaps millions, think'.

have a drink at the same
time. (It was better today
because Ella wasent there)
My school is realy trafic
at the moment, theres a
realy horrid girl in my
class called kerry whose
always beating up people
(I hate her). Im going to
Daddys & Madhus house
tomorrow. I cant wait. I thin
Madhus so beautiful and
daddys so handsome &
thin. I thinl my favourit
Best friend is probebly
Daisy, though I dont play
with her. She seems to

1

Taper in the rushing wind: moments of insight

Recently during a memoir class, one of my students asked about structure, and how difficult it is to pin down at the start of a project. She had been thrown by a mentor telling her she needed a distinct beginning, middle and end. I said I try to free myself from thinking about a linear or chronological structure in the early stages of writing, because structure often finds *itself*, not the other way around, particularly when writing memoir. Instead, I focus on 'moments', those memories that have resonated, and which open a door into some deeply felt meaning and deeper understanding. Every individual piece of writing demands its own shape, and we find that shape by paying attention to the moments that have defined us, and those that won't leave us alone.

There is an image that comes to me at odd times, still persistent. It was the inspiration for a novel that I wrote some years ago. It is a memory of sitting at a large wooden table in the dining room of a house in Cornwall that perches on the edge of a cliff. I am with a woman, an artist, who is a couple of generations older than me. We are drinking tea and talking about marriage. The room is brown in hue, with odd art works, but it is the view through the window that comes back most clearly. It is grey and green, and shining: the grey of the rocks is granite cut through with slate, the garden is overgrown and the sea beyond is teal green. There are flying balls of foam in the image too, from the waves that break on to the rocks, and the sound of the sea and wind is constant and calming. I see myself sitting at the table, the dappled light on my hands, but I remember that I was at an angle to the window, which is further obscured by ivy. So how did I see so much? It is my imagination that fills in the gaps. At high tide the sea is so close it might possibly break into the living room, steal the table where I sit and the bentwood chairs and stained old sofas, the quirky paintings and lampstands.

But, also, I am left with a feeling: when I am stressed or overwhelmed it bubbles up into my consciousness as a refuge, and I hold on to it as a premonition. I remember that in that moment of the past, when I sat talking to the woman who is an artist, I imagined that I might one day live there, or a place that was similar. I might one day be the older woman offering tea to a younger woman who is on the brink of leaving her husband. Perhaps this young lady is staying in a small house on the headland on her own, just as I was some eight years ago. Would I tell the younger woman – as this older lady told me – that it's better to stay and endure? 'You learn to live separate lives, to co-exist,' said the woman, alone in this beautiful big house perched on a cliff, alone to paint, while her husband was elsewhere. 'If you are an artist,' she said, 'the stability allows you to focus on your work.' I wanted that stability and that space to engage with my writing more than anything else, but I didn't want to live a half-life. What if I said something different to that young lady? What if I told her that, despite the pain, sometimes it's better to leave. That it won't be easy. What if true artistic freedom means breaking what is known, and building stability anew?

In Virginia Woolf's personal writing she explores what she calls 'moments of being'. In her essay 'Sketches from the Past', she writes that so much of life is a series of moments of non-being, 'the broken vacuum cleaner; ordering dinner; writing orders to Mabel; washing; cooking dinner; bookbinding', unconsciously going about the tasks of the day, as if wrapped in cotton wool. Occasionally we experience a 'violent shock' of revelation. These, according to Woolf, are the 'moments of being' when one feels the effects of an event deeply and reflectively. 'Something happened so violently that I have remembered it all my life,' she writes.

Exceptional moments are those that reveal something greater than the events themselves, some deeper meaning or wisdom. This might be a sense of powerlessness felt as a child, or a profound discovery, connecting with a presence that has always been there but obscured by the daily demands of life. In the example above, I had a clear sense that I wanted to be an artist, but that I didn't know if I could be the artist I wanted to be if I wasn't being true to myself. When Woolf witnesses a plant and its spread of leaves, she has a strong sense of how it is part of the earth, and part of a whole. She knows she should file away this discovery, to explore later, that it will be useful to her in some way. I wonder if my image of Cornwall returns to me in its attempts to be understood.

It is only now, writing it down and thinking through its significance, that I am beginning to understand it as a moment of being, of insight into myself and life itself.

Are there moments from your past that return to you? Perhaps they have lingered longer in the memory or even taken on a life of their own, compared to other memories that have been easily forgotten. They prick you because they are important; they make you stop and think and feel. Are they moments that reveal something to you, an inner wisdom that makes itself known, or are they moments when you felt alive and connected to the greater story, your purpose for living, your relationship with the world? They 'quicken the energy within you' as the psychoanalyst James Hollis notes. Maybe they are sad and painful, or maybe they are joyful. Or perhaps there is something about them that is not fully processed, that remains urgent in its need to be understood. They are the events that have pierced the featureless everyday because they hold meaning. They are 'moments of insight', a taper in the rushing wind.

You know those images that bubble up when you are in reverie, when driving the car, or out on a walk? We don't always notice them, and part of being a writer is learning to recognise the significance in these passing thoughts or feelings, or their associations, and to write them down. Capture them in a notebook, or on your phone. This is when the hard work starts, because as writers we must grab hold of what otherwise might be ephemeral, and ask ourselves, why? What if? It is when we stop and dig, turn the earth over, adding light and oxygen to what lies beneath, looking deeper and longer than we might have ever looked before, that new life will grow.

The taper is a still point in a world that rushes at us from all sides, hijacking our attention, via the internet, social media, news of wars, genocide and corrupt leaders, our responsibilities to put food on the table, to supply for our children, to simply earn enough to live. The taper waits to be lit, and the flame must remain despite the rush of wind, or better still be fuelled by the wind's oxygen and made to grow. The flame, or moment, or meaningful memory, however you might describe it, is the greatest antidote to the blank page.

One such image that haunted me for many years, as I mentioned earlier, was what became the beginning of an essay, which was published by Aeon and later developed into my memoir *Sins of My Father*. The image is of me and my brother standing on Hampstead High Street with our father, the first time we saw him after he had left his family and disappeared to India for six months. I was six and my brother was eight. Our father was dressed in a purple vinyl mix tracksuit, with nylon gaiters, and had a wooden beaded mala around his neck, a photograph of a bearded guru in a plastic wooden-framed disc at its centre. This was Bhagwan Shree Rajneesh, of whom my father was a devotee. As I picture it, I was wearing a duffel coat and my brother was wearing a Doctor Who scarf. Perhaps this image stayed with me because my father looked so different, a glazed and bemused look in his eyes. We hadn't seen him in a long time. But it is more likely because of what he said to us: looking otherworldly and dressed in clothes he never would have worn before he disappeared, he told me and my brother he had been reborn, that our father as we knew him was no more.

This was a moment of awakening for a six-year-old girl. My dad now existed in another universe that I could not reach, somewhere exotic and unimaginable. He had a girlfriend, someone other than my mother. He'd had some kind of epiphany. He had changed. Was this the moment my father ceased to be a father to me? Maybe. Something was revealed to me that was beyond the familiar, predictable world in which I existed. Perhaps also it was a moment of wisdom in this little girl, because I remember looking at my brother in disbelief as if our father had been possessed, taken hostage; he was acting something out, standing on someone else's stage. This was a feeling I was to have many times over the years that followed.

The significance of the moment when I met my father on the street slowly dawned on me through the process of writing it down. 'It's the shock-receiving capacity that makes me a writer,' Virginia Woolf reflects. The ability to take notice and to pay attention. 'The shock is at once in my case followed by the desire to explain it.' Through writing, I began to study the moment's emotional significance, and how it linked with other events from my childhood, and the story began to show itself. Studying this moment, returning to it again and again in my writing, an emotion was revealed to me: a predominant feeling I had as a child, an ineffable sadness and humiliating neediness in the snatched time I had with my dad. What if the sadness I often felt when with him in the months and years after this experience all started here when our father in effect disowned us as his children? As a child I was perplexed by my sadness, my inability to hush my noisy grief, but having this realisation as a writer who was driven to return to the past, I could start to see the problem was not actually mine, and so began a journey of regeneration.

This moment in Hampstead was important, to me personally but also in my writing, so I had to make it work hard for me: part of that involved manipulating details to unveil the deeper meaning. It's not simply that the moment reveals character or story, but also it must be a dramatic moment, something intriguing, which begs to be discovered; that our father had one foot on and one foot off the kerb, that there was a shaft of light, that he stared off towards the horizon. You will not remember every single detail of moments from the past, but by studying the emotional significance, you can conjure images that give concrete form to what otherwise is ephemeral, emotional, transitory.

It is our role as writers to have a conversation with our reader in a language they understand, and one way of doing this is to set the emotions alight in sensory detail, so that they can be felt. Writers are communicators, whose skill is measured by how clearly and memorably they can translate raw experience into story and make it relatable to the easily distracted reader. In committing this moment to the page, in taking time to help its transformation from memory into something new, both tangible and indelible, the writer allows the story to begin its evolution, and its separation from its creator. It takes on a life of its own, hopefully to alchemise again in the imagination of the reader in relation to their own experience; or by introducing something entirely and fascinatingly new. We hope that our writing will be a gift, a glimmer of wisdom perhaps, something appreciated and something learned.

If written well, this event might be as transformative to its reader as it was for its author and narrator.

Once you've written down those key moments that are important to you, which of them quickens your pulse and makes your heart race? Those episodes that spring from the page against those that feel forced? Because these will be the moments that matter most to you. They might be the most difficult to articulate, but their energy, however painful or volatile, will bring drama to the page. This is a good place to start. Those are the moments that hold story because plot evolves from a writer's attempt to confront and to understand. Questioning and probing are a memoir's blood, giving it a living presence on the page.

A story takes time to grow from idea into something viable; for many it can take years before a memoir comes into being. The best memoirs are deeply rooted in questions around psychology and our understanding of ourselves and of the human condition in a complex world which shifts and changes, resisting certainties and absolutes. The process is often intuitive, which is why it would not be possible to teach a university module on 'genre memoir'. The memoir that I might choose to write is so closely linked to the emotion I am exploring, from my highly subjective point of view, at a particular moment in time, that this memoir could be written only by me. It is deeply personal. If a personal story is shoe-horned into a preconceived structure it risks not being true to the seed from which it has grown, and therefore not being believable. And honesty and establishing trust are a memoirist's oxygen, however unbelievable a sequence of events may seem to be. Just as we cannot predict the path of any given life, I believe we cannot really predict the course of a memoir before a first draft.

It is this personal aspect that draws me to memoir, and I find myself underlining sections of text in the memoirs I read – those that move me or are revealing some deeply felt emotion or wisdom. I realise looking back at these that they are often 'moments of being'. In Noreen Masud's memoir about her search for solace and relief from her Complex Post-Traumatic Stress Disorder, *A Flat Place*, the landscape opens to her at Morecambe Bay. It 'looked like heaven', and she realises what she thought was water is actually land, perfect in its silvery flatness. This moment stays with the reader because it is so profound for Masud; that when observing the flat landscape, 'gradually the noise in my head quietened ... I could feel it in my forehead and my ears. With clean air on all sides of my body, I was outlined; I was given shape.' There are plenty more moments like this in Masud's memoir, as she discovers on her pilgrimage of flat landscapes around the UK – Orford Ness, Cambridgeshire Fens, Orkney – that they remind her of a flat place inside herself, away from the jangling intrusiveness of how she had to live as a child.

When I spoke with Masud she told me how she struggled at first to imagine *A Flat Place* as a memoir, because it had no story, in the traditional sense, or not the type of story she or I might teach our students in a creative writing class: Aristotle's Unified Plot Structure, for instance, shaped like a triangle, starting with an inciting incident and rising to a climax, and falling towards a resolution. What she was describing was flat, with no central point of focus, no single event to spring from or to return to. But she did have an emotional connection to place, and one that resonated deeply with a profound part of herself. From a young age, driving to school through a frantic Lahore with its traffic, donkey carts and street sellers, she'd wait for the moment when the world opened to an expanse of huge empty fields, 'We'd cross from city into fairy tale. And, every morning, no one noticed but me.' Seeing these open fields, she felt a profound sense of relief and freedom, in stark contrast to her daily life that was cramped and chaotic with her three sisters and mother, locked up in a house by her father, who obstructed their view of the world with chicken wire on the windows.

A Flat Place is a book about exile, post-colonialism and growing up under patriarchal rule, but it's also about the relief of finding a place to understand and where to feel understood. The flat landscapes become the focus, the framework, the holding space for the more difficult and nebulous stuff of emotion. Masud told me: 'I made the decision not to tell a story which seems like a turning-point in my life – the meat of "what happened to me" ... but that silence became an asset in the end. It allowed me to be straight with readers – to say to them: if I told this story, you'd think it was the point, the "peak" in the bare landscape to focus on gladly. But it's not the point. I'm going to withhold it. And you might have to cope with that, and to think about how it makes you feel, to have to sit with a story with no centre. Which is what I have to do as a person with Complex Post-Traumatic Stress Disorder.'

Significantly, in her book, Masud refers to *Moments of Being* by quoting Woolf's defining memory of being at St Ives, hearing the waves breaking behind a yellow blind. She hears the 'blind draw its little acorn across the floor as the wind blew the blind out', and asks of herself: what is *my* foundational memory? As Woolf writes, 'if life has a base that it stands upon, if it is a bowl that one fills and fills and fills – then my bowl without a doubt stands upon this memory', and Masud's life 'stands on those empty fields in Lahore'. The flat landscape gives meaning to a world that made no sense to the young Noreen. A space opened, and she felt at peace, and at points of crisis in her adulthood she has been drawn back to these landscapes. *A Flat Place* is a book born from a defining 'moment of insight', whose structure and shape reflects an emotional state held in that moment, both relief and discomfort, in its open and authentic state. The enduring flame in the rushing wind, so to speak.

One perfect piece of creative non-fiction that demonstrates such moments of insight in condensed form is Alice Walker's short essay 'Beauty: When the Other Dancer Is the Self'. In only seven pages, it captures a transformative moment in Walker's life. It is made up of moments – or scenes – as building blocks, a fine example of showing and not telling. There are simple moments that make up scenes, illustrating points in Walker's childhood as the youngest of eight children, and the innate racism and sexism a young black girl experiences in 1940s Southern counties. And there are key moments from which the essay pivots.

When I ask my students to identify these key 'moments', the obvious one – spoiler alert! – is when Alice's brother accidently shoots a pellet gun at her and the bullet hits her eye, which has lifelong consequences to her sight but also to her sense of self. But I tell my students to look again. This is a key moment, of course, without which this essay would not exist – but is it more an inciting incident, the moment of no return, when what came before is changed for ever? If we are to identify instead a 'moment of being' as Woolf defines it, that holds within it the potential for wisdom and insight beyond itself, the students point out the moment at the end of the essay when Alice Walker's toddler daughter gazes up at her mother. Walker tells us that her daughter is nearly three and how every day she watches a television programme called 'Big Blue Marble' which begins with a picture of the earth like the moon, blue and white and full of light. Walker is prepared for her daughter to be frank and cruel about her damaged eye, as children are prone to be, but instead her daughter surprises her: 'Mommy, there's a *world* in your eye.' And then she says, gazing up at her, 'Mommy, where did you *get* that world in your eye?'

This, my students suggest, is the moment of insight because it is the point for the writer when 'the pain left', a lifetime of pain, in her realisation when she looks in the mirror that there *is* a world in her eye and it is possible to love that same eye, 'for it had taught me of shame and anger and inner vision'. Her daughter's love and acceptance give Walker permission to love herself. Walker then dreams of a dancer who is the other version of herself, and who gives the essay its reason for being.

When I taught this recently, a student drew my attention back to the seemingly random addition of a poem at the essay's centre. The poem is called 'On Sight' and starts 'I am so thankful I have seen the desert'. And the student asked: is the poem there because it illustrates that *what* Walker sees, or more importantly *how* she sees, is what makes her a poet? *Yes!* Thanks to my student I now recognise that this is an important discovery for Walker, and a way that she can finally shake off the legacy of a doctor's insensitive comment that 'eyes are sympathetic' and if one is blind the other will most likely follow, and her fear that she will be left with no sight at all. This analysis also helps dig the poem's roots into the essay, because it links to Walker's realisation towards the end of the narrative that inner vision is as important as literal vision, that her blind eye wasn't simply a loss, a hindrance, but instead has taught her this. (I also love Walker's boldness at dropping a poem at the centre of an essay, with no real explanation as to why it is there.) Walker's sense of self improves as the essay progresses; we see her grow with confidence with every paragraph until the surprising interaction with her daughter at the end. And each time I read this essay, I wonder whether these realisations came to her through living, or through writing, or perhaps it was both.

In all the examples above, we witness a greater understanding of life or the human condition coming into being, what Virginia Woolf calls 'the real thing behind appearances', and which Phillip Lopate writes is 'the underlying shape of experience … not purely subjective, but which wait[s] patiently to be brought to the surface'. What if we all have a latent wisdom, and it is just a matter of discovering it? We simply need to create the right environment so that our inner life coheres with the life we are living. And what if writing helps us do this? On reflecting that 'one's life is not confined to one's body and what one says and does; one is living all the time in relation to certain background rods and conceptions,' Virginia Woolf writes: 'Mine is that there is a pattern hid behind the cotton wool .... I prove this, now, by spending the morning writing, when I might be walking, running a shop, or learning to do something that will be useful if war comes. I feel that by writing I am doing something far more necessary than anything else.'

If we are to believe Woolf and Lopate, we should see that these moments of insight are beyond ourselves, even. What if the artist is a cipher, a medium, for the greater business of meaning making? 'The whole world is a work of art; that we are part of the work of art,' writes Woolf. This takes the memoirist beyond simply finding words to tell a personal story; it takes us into the realm of philosophy and metaphysics; the artist as 'truth-sayer' (in as much as there is one guiding truth), the taper in the rushing wind. The young Noreen, cramped in the back of the car with her squabbling sisters, was the only one who noticed the flat fields. She was given the gift of noticing, and the creative powers to explore their significance. Reflecting on this, I wrote in my notebook: *in that moment we hold the whole world in our hands.* Do you see how important writing is? How the personal goes so far beyond a single skin?

If we believe this, then 'moments of being' exist despite us, embedded in the strata of lived experience, as ancient and sacred as mysterious standing stones. If the story is already there, and it is simply a writer's job to tap into its wisdom, it should be simple, right? But in our busy lives this can sometimes feel impossibly difficult. I remember at the start of the pandemic when everyone was in a heightened state of anxiety at this monster virus that was threatening to take over our lives – and did for a time – there were conversations online about how difficult it was to write. It felt impossible to enter into the well of ourselves in order to produce anything of value when the energy everyone was experiencing was thin and agitated, incapable of that deep absorption we had previously taken for granted. Thankfully that state of fight or flight did pass, but it was helpful to understand the effects stress has on creativity. We can create this space in ourselves by prioritising our writing, an envelope of time in the day preserved just for that. For me, it is first thing in the morning when I really try not to book any meetings or do the work that half my head can get away with doing later in the day.

But more broadly, perhaps we also need to design a life that allows it. When I finally left my marriage, I made a commitment to myself that I would make up for the disruption and the pain I had caused by building a positive life, with a man I loved, but who also helped me become a better writer, more in touch with myself. I did not want the distraction of a marriage that took all my energy just to make it work. I wanted to love with ease, but I also wanted to make art honestly; I believed that if I lived honestly, my energies would be focused, and the rest would follow. I just so happened to make a new life with another writer, and we share a sensibility and belief that writing is a necessary art, not as a commercial venture, but to better understand the self, and also to connect with others.

Soon after we met, he told me of a TEDx talk he had presented on this very topic and the influence of the *Naṭya Sastra*, classical Sanskrit drama, on his own creative practice. I tucked myself up in bed and watched him describe how you give up your head and with it your judgements, your expectations, your ambitions, and comparisons, all those societal pressures, and you give yourself to creativity and to form. By doing this you connect with what is really there, rather than the abstract or ephemeral. Finding the true form of structure in writing is 'not between form and formlessness,' he tells me. 'It is between mechanical and intuitive form.' When you touch on the meaning or what matters to you, your writing will tell you what form it should take.

Writing comes from within, the feeling self, from the heart; the hard work is mining the self, to tap into the complexity of existence, beyond one's everyday self. When we give ourselves over to our writing – when we truly give ourselves up to it, entering the 'flow state' when we lose all sense of who we are, what time it is, what is happening around us, we create art that should draw our readers into a similar state. In *The Good Story* by Arabella Kurtz and J. M. Coetzee, Coetzee recalls listening to the radio and a live performance by the pianist Angela Hewitt, and how she 'exposed herself to the music, and through her we were in turn exposing ourselves to it, letting it take us over'. He goes on to say that 'for the duration of the performance we were, so to speak, one soul, united in – I can't find a better word – love'. Coetzee refers to a communal experience – a performer with an audience – but writing that comes from the heart can conjure a similarly powerful response in its reader.

To bring something to life on the page, the writer needs to re-enter the experience, with as much intensity as if they were experiencing it again, with an intended result of what Aristotle described in his *Poetics* as an 'imitation [of life] that works through action'. If actions are dramatised with sufficient craft, the reader might well also feel these emotions, or access those that might have otherwise been suppressed. Catharsis is possible in the reader because it has happened in the writer. The sculptor Barbara Hepworth speaks of how carving stone is intimately related to waves hollowing a cliff, to the cavities in a human body, and how she is part of each sculpture she carves. She tells us she must 'feel my sculpture in my whole body'. If she gives the whole of herself, the sculpture holds the essence of Hepworth, who stands in for humankind. The sculpture itself blends with the landscape in which it stands. As with memoir, the relationship becomes symbiotic.

Many of us walk around in a daze of inattention, avoiding looking at the world around us, but also truthfully at ourselves. Socrates believed that the examined life is the most valuable life, that we should not only be aware of ourselves, but also question and reassess our actions and beliefs. But this takes hard work and a deep engagement with the self; it also takes courage to step into the imaginary realm and let the writing open our consciousness. How do we achieve this? All writing teachers tell us to take away distractions, to close the door and lock away the phone, which of course is the first step. But it might also help to return to a place in the imagination where you once felt at one with yourself, or had glimmers of an inner wisdom. This might be a landscape that resonates, where you spent your childhood, and perhaps is foundational to you discovering yourself as a writer or an artist. Woolf had St Ives, and her childhood memories, which brought her closer to her mother who had died when she was young. Noreen Masud had the flat landscapes in Lahore, that gave meaning to a world that made no sense to her. Or perhaps it is a literal space, where you can go inwards, and enter the deep caverns of yourself. 'A room of one's own' as Woolf famously wrote, which could simply be your bed with the door closed, or a café. There have been times in my life where the only quiet space I have found has been a toilet cubicle, or my car.

But I also have a landscape, similar to Woolf's St Ives, which speaks to a more creative part of myself: that same coastline in Cornwall where I visit each year with my children, but also visit alone, to make the space to work on a book, or to simply walk and think and come back into myself. It features in the last chapter of my memoir. There are many moments captured in that final chapter that are rooted in that place, when I was swimming in the sea, walking along a path and hearing the distant sound of the waves, standing on a promontory in among the warming sun and chamomile, and receiving a scent-filled hug. They were all with the man for whom I'd risked the stability of my life, for a second chance of happiness.

When I sit with these memories, I realise there are many more, and some go far back to when I spent my summers in North Cornwall as a child, and where my grandparents lived for a time. An expanse of beach, sand dark with wet, a stinging wind, and me, having stripped off to my underwear, with my mum and her sisters, emerging from the sea to my grandmother greeting me and wrapping me in her nylon petticoat. I remember the texture and how it was cold and slippery against my skin, a barrier to anything being absorbed. But I also remember my granny laughing and my gratitude to her for attempting to dry me. This moment holds my grandmother so succinctly, her awkward empathy, always present but often clumsy. She had a hard hand in affection that cracked against mine with its gnarled knuckles and rings. But she was a constant and strong presence, a pioneer who grew up in hardship in South Africa before meeting my grandfather and travelling to the UK with six of their eight children to start a new life. She was supremely competent and practical, but also artistic. She chose me on that beach to attempt (and fail) to dry me with her petticoat, which is perhaps why this image stays with me. When I re-imagine this moment now it speaks of my bond with her, but it also reminds me that Cornwall is important to me, as it was to her and my wider family. I cannot return blindly when I go camping with my children each year. It is a place that matters. Not just to me, but also to them, as they grow and nurture their own relationship with this part of the world, generation after generation. I feel the urge now to file away this thought and revisit it another time, open my heart and mind to its potential story.

It also helps me reflect on how the landscape might be a motif for my essential nature. Both smooth and fractured, calm and questioning. How here there is beauty in conflict and imperfection, and risk is inevitable. It feels real. A simple walk from the house where I stay involves brambles, stinging nettles and catching your skin and clothes on thorns. Here I can connect with the precariousness of life, the more natural dangers, which somehow satisfies a restlessness in my temperament to agitate stability and create trouble where there is none. The eye is drawn to the horizon, but also to the constant movement of the water, its surface ever-changing, the subtlety of colour, the thunder of the sea. And when I look again, the horizon has been obscured by mist and cloud. There is nothing predictable about any of it, except for its majesty, its timelessness and solidity, and the fact that I respect it deeply. A space opens inside me, a white light, expansive and pure. I sit down and write.

Try this:

1. If you're struggling to find your story, try some automatic writing. Set a timer for three minutes and tell the critical part of the brain to shush, and start writing freely, without stopping. Your prompt is: *moments I remember*. Start with – 'I remember' and see where it leads you. Try to get more than one specific moment if you can, jumping from one to the next to the next. Your pen might linger over some more than others; you might even feel an itch to stop and explore. Move on if you can. At this stage I don't want you to think about why you're selecting these moments over other moments. Just write down the first thing that comes to mind. What you will most likely find is that one memory will lead to another memory to another – either good or bad, like 'dredging up an old boot with things attached to it …' says the poet and memoirist Clare Best. Before you know it you will have more incidents than you know what to do with.

2. Choose one or two of the moments you have noted down, those that interest you the most – that get your heart racing! – and write down every little physical detail you remember from this particular event. This is still just in note form. No one needs to see these notes, so relax and let yourself go. Where were you, what were you wearing, what was the weather like? What could you see? Smell? Feel? Were there any

particular noises? Try to engage with your senses. If you can't remember this much detail, let your imagination kick in a bit. You are allowed to fill in the gaps.

3. Now, I want you to refine these observations, and engage with your lens. The lens is not only you, but the emotional tone of the moment. Try to hold the moments in an emotional space in your mind. Was your mood subdued or heightened in this past event? Would you have been aware of those details that were around you, or only of the person who stood before you? Go through your list and cross out those details that you might not have seen in that particular emotional state. Here I want you to record only the specific things that would have attracted your attention in that moment, and what they look like. For example, a bed has a different meaning to someone who has been up all night caring for an ailing mother, compared to someone who's been bedridden for three weeks and is finally feeling well enough to go back to work. Jot all these observations down.

4. Next, I want you to engage with your reflective voice. Take the same one or two specific moments that you want to focus on and take your time to think about why they are important to you. Why do you think these memories have stuck with you all this time? Write down your reflections. What you should have now is the addition of hindsight: even if these events happened to you as an adult, you will have the benefit of having had some distance from them to be able to see them differently from how you viewed them in the moment.

5. Now write your moment, as you remember it. As close to how you think it happened as you can. But engage with all the senses as you write it and attempt to make it into a working scene. Add dialogue if you want, and characterisation, too, and pay attention to detail and setting. Think about your moment leading somewhere else. Shape the narrative so that it becomes a segue to another scene, but also try to make it self-contained.

One more exercise if you're really keen!

Choose a place that means something to you, as I wrote about Cornwall above. It can be a country, or a city, or a town, or a neighbourhood, or zoom in even more – a particular street, or a house, or even simply a room in that house – what about the kitchen, or your childhood bedroom? And I want you to engage with your senses and to list a minimum of 15 concrete smells, sounds, sights, textures and tastes related to this place. If I was back on that beach in Cornwall, it would be the chill of the wind on my bare flesh when I stepped from the water, the smell of bladderwrack and rotting fish, the seagulls cawing, and maybe a dog barking at his shadow, the feel of the cold and wet sand between my toes. I might have a taste of comfort, the chatter of my teeth, and feel in my mouth the words of appreciation for my grandmother when she attempts to wipe sticking sand from my achingly cold limbs. Or maybe it's the memory in my mouth of sweet warmth, when I think of the hot chocolate she will make for me when we get back to her house.

Laura is making a cup of tea
Why is she making a cup of tea?
Because she's tired
Why is she tired?
Because she had a row with her husband
Why did she have a row?
Because she's jealous
Why is she jealous?
What does jealousy mean?
Because her father had an affair
She doesn't trust.

Deep desire: to trust.
Why not? = Sense of betrayal
This is what the story must resolve

This relates to the PhD - understanding the
motivation - the psychology going deeper
in order to explore that - curiosity. Asking
questions creating that safe space in
which to take risks. — my nonfiction
student comment about my way of teaching

2

Snow in August: when memory collides with the imagination

Here is a memory: my partner, Robin, and I are at Barbara Hepworth's house in St Ives listening to a guide speaking about Hepworth's life. It is summer, breezy and white, and we join others in a circle – sandals, loose trousers, sunglasses perched on heads. I don't remember if my children were there, but I have a hazy image of them on the periphery. I do remember photos of Hepworth smoking, and huge slabs of rock in the garden, enormous and exotic plants. I remember the vitality of her studio, creepers covering the walls, her tools haphazard on counters as if she had just nipped out for a fag. I remember being moved by the story of her son dying and how the grief was so bad she lost the ability to work. I wrote scraps of observation in my notebook: *high ceilings and big windows, all shades of white, and beautiful light;* and something curious: *Robin and I are standing stones, timeless and present, inert and listening.*

My memories from that afternoon are fragmented, fleeting, patchy, but they are mostly driven by feeling, and a sense that our visit had been important. Robin would later write a play that featured a grieving female sculptor at its centre; I would quote from Hepworth in my teaching, how placing a figure in the landscape changes our relationship with what we see. How the human form animates nature. But what if I wanted to include this event in a memoir, the literal telling of a couple visiting a gallery, interacting with each other and the surrounds, two people in an artist's studio? I have retained so little actual detail. Can I recall enough of the experience of being there to write convincingly about it?

I have the observations I jotted in my notebook, but I also have my imagination. When I close my eyes, I find myself conjuring images: I see our bodies blend with the walls, cavities and hollows opening; we *are* those standing stones. By making notes of what I saw, and what I felt, I have created a new kind of reality, one that is rooted in the ideas of an artist who inspires me, but which have expanded and become personalised in my imagination. As a memoirist I must mine those images, and uncover their meaning, looking for the emotion that waits to be revealed.

But I must not fabricate, as that would throw into question the validity of the entire form. Writers owe it to memoir as a genre to be honest, otherwise why not simply call it fiction? And memory is crucial to memoir as a form. But when memory is such a faulty, fallible thing, so inexact in nature, so essentially subjective, and when it so often returns to us as a feeling, you must give yourself permission to let it expand in your imagination. Writing memoir – at least in a first draft – then becomes an opportunity to ask questions of the images that return to you. To write them, spend time with them, and begin their interpretation. It's not simply what and how you remember that is interesting, it's also what and why you forget.

When we were at the gallery, we bought a book – *Barbara Hepworth: Writings and Conversations*, a collection of Hepworth's published writing and interviews. In it, Hepworth speaks of how ideas are 'born through a perfect balance of our conscious and unconscious life and ... are realised through this same fusion and equilibrium'. That art is made both from what is material, and from intuitive imagination. But this fusion also, she writes, makes up a life force: 'I, the sculptor, am the landscape. I am the form and I am the hollow, the thrust and the contour.' She writes extensively about how in her sculpture she endeavours to find the 'evocative symbol affirming these early and secure sensations'. What she follows is often the 'feeling of the magic of the man in the landscape', inspired by someone she might have spotted going about their day, 'whether pastoral or a miner ... or the "single form" of a mill girl moving against the wind with her shawl wrapped round her head and body.' And this form takes on a new shape in her imagination: 'In my dreams I see people rising out of the rush of the tides,' she writes. As a direct response, Hepworth's sculptures have the appearance of rocks smoothed by the sea, and groups of people in relationship with each other, often a synthesis of contradictory forces, the personal and the universal, emotional and physical. While the starting point is symbol, it's Hepworth's connection with her feeling, instinctive self that makes art.

Hepworth is a lesson for all memoirists, as they move between different states in their writing: the materiality of rock might be the facts – for instance, what is proven – and the intuitive self finds expression in the flux and inexact nature of imagination and feeling. Part of being a writer is trusting your feeling self and listening to the messages it sends you. Curiously, thinking back to that day in St Ives, when I let my imagination free, I see a huge rock protruding from the centre of Hepworth's studio, but when I look at images on the internet I see only small-scale rocks, half hewn and finished sculptures, and I wonder if the mass and heft of the rock reflect a feeling I had of being dwarfed by the scale and greatness of her talent, her clear and unimpeded commitment to her work. The rock becomes a symbol of the impression Hepworth left on me. This is my interpretation.

And what of the merging of me and Robin with the environment? Is it a sign of some deeper truth that moved me, about the close alignment between an artist's life and their art, and by extension between art and those who witness it? That we are all in relationship with each other. If so, it makes sense for me to write that afternoon in imaginary, embodied prose, rather than telling it straight – particularly as I lack so much factual information. Hepworth's art is so intuitive, after all.

After a lifetime of keeping a notebook and journal, I realise that they are also 'born through a perfect balance of our conscious and unconscious life', of experience – what we observe – and of reflection: our thoughts, feelings and revelations, which often come to us in hindsight. When I stop to flick through the pages of such a notebook, I find the parts of my past I was moved enough by to record: quotes from a book, a moment documented, a conversation had – which, without intention, have become crucial research for writing memoir (or in fact, fiction!). There are also many pages of my workings-out of feelings: a thought that suddenly bubbles up, something unresolved, and an attempt to explain it.

When I was writing my memoir, I asked my mother to fill in the years before I was born, to get a better grasp of her relationship with my father, the clothes they wore in the 1970s, small details like the bouquet of flowers her mother thrust into her hands on her wedding day, cut from the garden just that morning. Reading back these notes I see the bouquet as a symbol of my grandmother's artfulness: immediate, unselfconscious. It is symbolic of character, but also of the naturalness of two young lovers marrying impulsively barely a year after they met. This detail, along with photographs, helps me conjure the image of a day I did not witness.

The notebook or journal becomes an important piece of evidence. It has both symbol (in my case, my mother's bouquet) and its hidden emotion (the ease and naturalness of my mother's family and the impulse of my parents' love). It is an archive, but it is also highly personalised. The way we store memory, and the way we record it in notebooks or diaries is particular to our individual per-sonalities and sensibility, our expectation, or past hurts and fears, because we notice only what moves us. In a journal we are free to be ourselves, and to nurture our voices, and our relationship to the world.

I urge my fellow memoirists and students to use their notebooks like a visual artist might in drawing sketches, dashing down observations of an evocative moment, significant of something deeper, a fragment to be remem-bered and perhaps used again. My memoir *Sins of My Father* started life as a series of memories written in the heat of the moment. I remember throwing myself down on the living-room sofa, and feverishly writing out the painful memories of the last time I saw my father, drunk, incontinent, which had existed in me for so long, incomprehensible, and unspeakable, like sediment. I had not known how to express it, let alone exorcise it, and the sediment had been rising and seeping out, affecting my life and my relationships. When my marriage started to fall apart, and I had no idea why, I turned to writing because I knew from past experience that it worked. And the slow, painful work of excavation began.

Through the writing, I began to understand how the events of that week were connected to other events in my life around that time. I recalled my father's phone call a few nights before my wedding, when he was drunk, a wreck, crying about how sorry he was and how he loved me, and I was curled up on my bed and the tears were so insistent I couldn't regulate my breathing. I had just had an all-body spray tan in preparation for my wedding – an uncharacteristic move for me! – and when I looked in the mirror there were tear streaks down my cheeks, which remained however much I tried to scrub them away. I wore the ghost of those tears on my wedding day. Although at the time it seemed just another tragi-comic incident in my life, in contemplation for my memoir it assumed symbolic power, a metaphor for my unrequited love for my father. The timing of his phone call, the effect it had on me and how I could not escape it were deeply revealing of the hold he had over me and how, in my tear-stained face, I carried that into the next stage of my life, so desperately trying to be free of him but tethered still, always in his shadow. My father ended up in intensive care during my honeymoon, and my husband and I had to cut our holiday short.

As memoirists we settle on this significant moment of illumination and then radiate meaning from its core. It may take some time before you have distance enough from the crisis to begin to find the meaning in experience, and how one event relates to another. I began to see that my story, for instance, had time at its centre. As a child I was often suspended in a state of waiting for my father to phone, or to write, or to turn up at our house, or to pick us up from the airport when we travelled to see him in Italy (if he ever actually did – we got the train more often than not, from Pisa to Florence, whether evening or night). I came to see that my role was simply to wait and to follow. Once I had identified this, I wrote a short piece about waiting, and selected only the memories that slanted towards this theme. There (and then), I had my structure.

What I learned from writing was that I was someone who arrived on time, and someone whom many people kept waiting. This was my truth, one which had manifested as an aspect of my personality. But what if we dig deeper into this concept? Was this pattern mine, or was there a fault in the fabric because of my father's neglect? Was this my story or had my story for all these years been determined by someone else's? The story begins to broaden and to shift. If you ask questions of your experience, you begin to see it in the context of other people's stories, a parent's influence, for instance, something that up until now was out of your hands. It becomes not so much fact, but circumstance. With this realisation comes a repat-terning of the past on your own terms, and a new story comes into being. On the page, but also in life. Writing down memory, and mining it for value and hidden meaning, your perspective alters and renews.

In my story, this repatterning coincided with a momentous shift in my own life and my consciousness. Having walked away from my marriage, I was looking for a way to build a new life of my own. In my hands I held a bowl that had been shattered into a million tiny pieces, and I had been given the chance to put those pieces back differently, to create a new shape, a different configuration. This was a kind of reinvention, but one that had to be handled with care.

When Robin and I tentatively went on our first dates, I turned to my notebooks and journals, either immediately or retrospectively over the months that followed, wanting to keep hold of the feeling, but also to keep myself in check. Some months later, I remembered back to when we had arranged to meet beneath the clock in Waterloo Station, and how I was early as usual, but for some reason had taken a wrong turn and walked across the wrong bridge, which was perplexing to me when I know London so well. This made me late, so I panicked and started running. I wrote how I had felt a blast of cold wind when I entered the station, and had ducked and slipped between crowds of people, my eye on the clock hanging from the ceiling, which clearly marked my lateness, its minute hand on 3, which was 15 minutes late! And there he was beneath it, his body relaxed, arms linked behind his back, his face calm. I flung my arms around his neck and kissed him, apologising. 'I am late!' I appeared to shout, and he held me, and nodded. 'You're late,' he said, and 'I enjoyed waiting for you.'

I wrote about how up to this point it had always been me, the waiter, and how, when I saw him waiting for me there beneath the iconic Waterloo clock, I had felt my heart surge, that the path before us had opened, the leaves of last autumn now mulched and starting to disintegrate. I wrote that I remember it being cold when we left the station, or maybe we simply found warmth in each other. He wore a black wool coat, which made him look like a bear, with me on his arm.

But what if I was wrong? What if it hadn't been cold that day? What if he had worn that big black coat another day – when we had sat on a bench on the Embankment and he had squashed a cup of coffee in his hand so hard that the lid had popped off and coffee spilled all over that same coat? I remember his bigness. I remember his warmth. It is this that I remember, beyond any small detail like a coat. But the coat becomes symbolic for both these things, from both the conscious and the unconscious, formed from memory and the imagination, a kind of touchstone for character and story.

For those of you who worry about getting the facts right, you can't do better than read Joan Didion. In her famous quote, 'Perhaps it never did snow that August in Vermont; perhaps there never were flurries in the night wind, and maybe no one else felt the ground hardening and summer already dead even as we pretended to bask in it, but that was how it felt to me, and it might as well have snowed, could have snowed, did snow,' she boldly follows her feeling self, and is explicit in her twisting of the facts. The emotion is the important thing here, and her honest connection with herself, a wholly subjective rendering of the *feeling* that summer was dead. She writes this in her essay 'On Keeping a Notebook', where she questions those details she has collected, privately, and how if she had been hung up with recording the facts alone, it would reflect 'an interest in reality' which, she tells us, she simply does not possess. Didion is a writer, after all, and writers are daydreamers. Writers honour their imaginations.

Didion keeps a notebook to 'remember what it was to be me'. And by sharing this aspect of her personality with us, her reader, she invites us in. We admire her for her honesty and her willingness to present herself as human, complex, faulty; after all, she tells us, 'keepers of notebooks are a different breed altogether, lonely and resistant rearrangers of things, anxious malcontents, children afflicted apparently at birth with some presentiment of loss'. Her arch humour and willingness to dissect herself is indeed refreshing.

Didion writes that in her recording of memory or what has moved her, she tells what others would call lies. But she is not pretending they are anything but, and here is the crux. In sharing the unreliability of memory, or the misremembering, she makes it the subject of her piece, but she also invites the readers to be complicit. Didion opens the intimate, private nature of the notebook to her audience – she treats them like friends – and her audience is touched that they are trusted to such a degree.

This acceptance of memory's fallibility is common in the more thoughtful memoirs I have read, those that raise fundamental questions about the slippery nature of memory and storytelling. After all, however close a piece of writing is to pure fact-based non-fiction, claiming to convey the truth, it still manipulates by creating a linear narrative compressing time, even using dialogue (which is not the same as conversation). Those memoirs that draw our attention to the artifice of storytelling are more truthful, perhaps, than those biographies which claim to replicate the factual, 'the real'.

A great example of a memoir that makes a point of the slippery subjective nature of memory is Hua Hsu's Pulitzer Prize-winning memoir *Stay True*, about friendship and identity, and the compulsive desire to document a brief relationship with a college friend after he is killed in a carjacking. Hsu has an urgent need to write down his memories of his friend Ken, but questions this motivation: is it to capture reality – 'I wrote out of a responsibility for our past' – or a kind of nostalgia, a search 'for treasured memories of better days' before the awful events of that summer. Or was it more about the future, as he states in an interview with the broadcaster Scott Simon? Was he trying to 'repair the world through writing', to 'imagine a different future ... the future that never came'? Was this an expression of his grief, and did the writing end up being a kind of eulogy?: 'a story that flattered the narrator, forcing grace and intention onto every strong memory. A self-consciousness that everything was combed with meaning, where friendship's casual rhythms rarely warranted this kind of scrutiny'. Was the writing simply attempting to pin meaning to something that was terrible and meaningless? 'When the only truth is it's fucked up the way it is sometimes.'

But the real truth in this memoir is not so much the memorialising of a lost friend and that friendship, but more Hsu's scrutiny of himself and his failings. An insecure adolescent in search of his own identity in 1990s California, the second-generation child of immigrant Asian parents, he does not feel represented by popular culture and therefore takes a position on the sidelines, defining himself by those things he rejects, including aspects of Ken's personality, which is more easy-going and accepting, and more easily American. Is his obsession with Ken more an obsession with the parameters and possibilities of himself? Paradoxically, his friendship with Ken opens up Hsu's world to accept and be accepted by others. In *Stay True*, Hsu reflects on how his journal contained his half of continued conversations with Ken after his death: his continued relationships with their mutual friends, the movies they would have gone to see together had he still been alive. He tells him about *The Matrix*, how it is a 'movie about unlearning our relationship to the world. What we considered real life was just a state of permanent dreaming.' He goes on to reflect on how writing offers a way of skipping out of the present, being more concerned with language than living. Hsu is ruthlessly honest, philosophical in his outlook. He does not take anything at face value. He doesn't simply write a story; he writes about why we tell stories.

Similarly, the poet Nick Flynn creates story from absence, and *Another Bullshit Night in Suck City* is a great example of how to write a story from scraps of evidence. In his memoir, he brings into being his father, a character who had left the family when Flynn was four and whom he only meets again in a homeless shelter where he works in his late twenties, when his father – homeless – stumbles in. 'If you asked me about my father then – the years he lived in a doorway, in a shelter, in an ATM – I'd say, *Dead*, I'd say, *Missing*, I'd say, *I don't know where he is.* I'd say whatever I felt like saying, and it would all be true.'

But Flynn has years of his father's letters sent from prison – albeit many of them boastful and fuelled by fantasy – and it is these letters, and Flynn's poetic imagination and wisdom to read between the lines, that form the backbone of this hybrid memoir about a man whom he never knew. 'Ten years of a father built entirely of his own crazy words.' Flynn makes the limitations of having little first-hand experience of his father work in his favour in that much of this narrative uses the scant particular to make a broader point about humanity. A chapter named 'Cloverleaf' starts with:

> The world's so large, each city full of cheap rooms, each room behind a door. Men lie in these rooms, press their bodies into mattresses, pull the shade in the morning, pace wide-eyed at night. Someone always comes along, picks you up. You have to end somewhere right? Damn near law of physics.

It is both his father's voice, his own voice and that of the everyman, homeless and destitute. Throughout the memoir, Flynn switches point of view, from specific first person, to second person when writing about his father, to the more universal third person. This works particularly well because one of the presiding themes throughout the memoir is Flynn's identification, or the active denial of his identification, with his father. As the daughter of an alcoholic who also became destitute, I was particularly moved by Flynn's fear that if he lets his father inside, 'I would become him, the line between us would blur, my own slow-motion car wreck would speed up.' When my students complain to me that they have nothing to write about, I tell them to go to the library to find this book.

Similar to Flynn, I had to find a way of writing about a father who had been mostly absent, both physically and emotionally, and I remember coming up against this in the early months, and thinking: how do I write about a man who spent so little time with me, who spent much of my life in active avoidance of his family and his children? By the end of his life, he had burned bridges with all his friends, so there were very few people to talk to about him. His parents were dead. I had lost contact with my stepmother, his second wife. The only people I could speak to were my brother, my mother and his sister, who had a damaged relationship with him. But, like Nick Flynn, I had artefacts.

My father was a writer and he wrote prolifically, and across many different genres: science fiction, poetry, memoir, novels, non-fiction coffee-table books. He had published a thinly disguised autobiographical novel, and had been writing a 'memoir about alcoholism' up until his death, both of which were illuminating (in ways he might not have intended). He had even – with unintentional irony – published a book on child-rearing! I had letters that he had sent my mother when they were together, and those he had sent me from when he lived in Italy, and drafts of all my letters I had sent in return, full of pain and longing, wanting to be back there with him. I had also kept his medical records from when he was in and out of intensive care in the last years of his life. These artefacts, along with my research, began to give narrative form to what previously had been memory in fragments.

But I also had to acknowledge myself as storyteller, beyond permanent witness. My father lived the last ten or so years of his life in California, which is where my memoir begins, just at the point of no return when he makes a decision that will seal his fate and lead him further down the rocky path of alcoholism. I had to picture him in his house the day he answered a suspicious email, on a day I had not been there. And so I am explicit in the text that I have to rely on my imagination. The very first two words of the prologue are 'I imagine'. And as the story continues, I am careful to remind the reader that this scene is being pieced together from my imagination. 'I was not there that fateful day in 2003, but I had visited the Christmas before, his first Christmas in the house and without his wife.'

This speculative element of the text had another effect too. It helped me slip between facts into areas that had not previously been explored, where I had new revelations that went deeper than the myths we had always told ourselves. By reading about 'his type', whether through books about addiction, or narcissism, or of men who had gone through the boarding-school system, I was able to empathise with him but also to objectify him. Somehow, it took away the personal hurt that he had done this to me, as it made him into a victim of his circumstances. The deeper I went into the research, the more my father became relatable, an everyman, the specifics of his struggles pointing to the universal. But more importantly, perhaps, I was also turning him into story, so much more than simple transcription and recollection of fact. Through the writing, researching and redrafting, he became a character in a drama of my creation, and I, for the first time, was in command.

There seems to be a certain level of 'knowing yourself' in this process, which sounds far easier than it is in practice. As human beings we are driven by our emotions, and it is not always easy to stand apart from ourselves and to see the deeper meaning in our actions. But to write convincingly about any character – whether yourself or another – that character must be well understood. Writing memoir helped me to explode the myths about myself and my father, and the anecdotes that we as his family had always told. It pushed me to question myself and my knee-jerk responses, and to engage with what the memoirist Mary Karr calls the 'noticing self'. In your writing, ask yourself, is there jealously beneath that quick and hot anger, is your return to the place of your childhood nostalgia or grief? Good memoir springs from pausing within a moment or situation in our lives and going deeper than perhaps we ever have before; to touch the sensory nerve of experience and to discover something more truthful, beyond those narratives we have lived by. 'One reason we might fail to know ourselves is that we don't want to know ourselves: or, at least, we only want to know ourselves if the knowledge will make us feel good,' writes Helena de Bres, in her illuminating *Artful Truths: The Philosophy of Memoir*. Perhaps it's not that we didn't see it: it's that we didn't want to see it.

At the start of each academic year, I tell my students to keep a journal and to carry it around with them always. As we saw earlier, this documents experience – essential for any writer – but it also helps develop voice, and more specifically the reflective voice. Anna Wilson, author of *A Place for Everything*, about her mother's late diagnosis of autism and how living with no diagnosis affected her growing up, tells me she has kept a diary since she was aged seven and will continue to keep one 'as long as I can hold a pencil'. She says she wouldn't have been able to write her memoir without journalling first – 'it would have been an almighty tangle' – and it was a way of getting her feelings out of the way, as well as recording important detail, 'when I was feeling most raw', which she would otherwise have forgotten.

Author of *Home Is Where We Start*, Susanna Crossman referred to her teenage journal when writing her memoir to similarly remind herself of detail, but also of voice, and the author and memoirist Dani Shapiro, in her marriage memoir, *Hourglass*, includes extracts from the journals she wrote decades earlier, as a way of returning to a former version of herself. Returning to the journal I wrote in my teens, I was moved (and a little bit embarrassed) by the self-consciousness in my formal language, and my transparent striving for maturity. I could also recognise moments where I was writing for the sake of writing, and those when I was driven by something more profound: when I stopped trying, and lost my self-consciousness or parodying, the writing tended to come alive, which was a lesson in creative writing itself.

We've seen how journals are important sources for research, but what if they are more than that? What if they help you find your memoir's structure? The poet and memoirist Clare Best shared with me the multiple uses of her journal. How she turned to it in the last two years of her father's life as a 'safe place' where she could explore and vent complex feelings, and to steady herself. Then later, she realised that the journal was more essential than that. For her memoir, *The Missing List*, it provided not only the timeline and a place to chart her emotional development, but also a 'personal scaffold through that difficult time of lived experience, and that journal then provided the scaffolding for the structure of the book'.

We all have images from our childhood that come back to us vividly, whereas events of yesterday merge into all the other events of the recent weeks. Memory experts say this is because so many experiences in our childhood were new, a novelty, whereas growing older, our attention is split between too many things, too many experiences are too easily forgotten. I read a piece by Alain de Botton, on how time distorts as we get older, not because it is speeding up but because we don't take so much notice of those things around us, because they no longer feel as new as they did when we discovered them for the first time. 'The more our days are filled with new, unpredictable, and challenging experiences, the longer they will feel. And conversely, the more one day is exactly like another, the faster it will pass by in a blur.' This isn't to say we all need to constantly pursue new experiences to make new memories; more that we can look at the experiences we have with new eyes.

One simple way to slow down time and to make memories is to pay attention to what you see around you when you do the usual walk to the local shops. Put away your worries (and your phone) and turn attention outwards – the world can always look fresh and new if you give it enough attention. Dr Charan Ranganath in *Why We Remember: The Science of Memory and How It Shapes Us* signposts attention and intention. In our increasingly noisy world of information clamouring for our attention, it is so easy to be distracted. Take a notebook with you and make a point of stopping and looking and making notes, recording those things you witness around you. This will also help develop your voice in the now, the person writing this memoir, compared to that of yesterday or going back further into childhood. We will expand on this dual perspective in the next chapter, 'From the static into the moving world', but it is important to acknowledge here that a point in the past will look one way to a middle-aged woman, and completely different to that same woman aged 20. A woman at the middle of her life may bring wisdom and compassion, compared to a young woman who is only just starting to see herself as separate from her parents, who may not yet feel the liberation of understanding and forgiveness.

But 'although we tend to believe that we can and should remember anything we want, the reality is we are designed to forget, which is one of the most important lessons to be taken from the science of memory,' Ranganath tells us. As writers we have to work hard to hold on to the important stuff, because everything is potential material, and the best memoirs have that special ability to reconfigure the past as if it were still happening. If we believe the science, we cannot rely on our memory alone.

If you're finding it too difficult to recall memories, spend an afternoon going through your photographs. These might bring up difficult emotions, but remember it is the photographs that we want to avoid – for fear of the feelings that will resurface in us – that hold the most story. Pause on those photographs if you're able to and take yourself back to that place. I did this in the early stages of writing *Sins of My Father*, looking back at iconic photographs of my childhood when my dad was still around. I found myself reading into his body language, how he positioned himself next to me. How my knees as a child sloped towards his, how his sloped away. Describe the image, what you see, but also what you feel.

Writing from photographs is also a good way of capturing character. The memoirist and poet Mark Doty does it beautifully in *Firebird* when introducing us to the characters of his parents. Looking at a photograph of his father as a boy he writes:

> He's appealingly good looking, not movie star looks but a sensuousness and a quality of alert presence which don't strike me as having much to do with the man as I've known him. It's the clarity of the large eyes, which look off to the right as though towards the future.

Looking at a photograph taken later, he reflects: 'In the next photograph the future has arrived; his smile and tilt of the head say that whatever it was that was coming is here, and good.' This leads him to a photograph of his mother, because of course it was his mother whom the boy in the first picture had been waiting for. He describes his mother and her perfect smile, 'beautiful, unchecked, no hesitation in it …' but here comes something intriguing:

> Her smile and her eyes don't quite align, the dazzle of one just so subtly opposing the depth of the other: delight and – what? Something withheld, not yet available to us? Something, unlike that smile, which is unwilling, unready to be known.

This is not simply Doty looking closely at what he observes; this is Doty writing from feeling and memory of a woman who was always slightly out of reach. His feelings about his mother, the lasting impression she has made on him, are as important as the facts of her existence, in the case of this memoir perhaps even more so. They are what create story. When Doty writes 'There's a particular hold love has over you when you're afraid of who you love', he holds the reader in his hands.

Try this:

1. A useful way into memory is to look at, or think your way back into, photographs from the past. If we are to believe that 'memoir seeks a permanent home for feeling and image', as stated by the memoirist Patricia Hampl, then there is so much more than just testimony or description. I find it useful to think of an onion, of peeling back the layers. There is the image itself: *where am I and with whom?* There is the emotion expressed – overtly or hidden: *What is the body language and facial expression?* And then the question of what is happening off stage? This is where the imagination kicks in, conjuring the detail of where we were and why. What happened before the image was taken, and what after? Memory's fallible nature is questioned here, as we can never be certain we get it right. What we imagine might be a composite of various different moments from various different points in time, but we can at least try to get the emotion right: capturing a moment of change in a girl's life, on a step at the back of the school, on the cusp of life. The imagination helps us find meaning in that image, digging for hidden emotion: a memoir's first drop of blood.

2. Is there a photograph that sits by your bed, or perhaps it is hidden in the bottom drawer of your desk, never to be looked at again? But what if you have a peek at it? A photograph tells many stories and is a good place to start. I often hear people tell me they could never

write memoir because their memory is shot, particularly as they get older and the gap between where they are now and their childhood or adolescence seems too big to traverse. But all we need is that prompt, or trigger, and as we saw in the previous chapter memory breeds memory breeds memory, until we have before us pages and pages of detail that we had no idea was hiding in the attic of the mind.

3. Find a photo, not just a portrait, but one that has two or more people in it, or something curious like an arm reaching into the frame, a teacup or a hat. Or maybe it is simply you, but you are standing on your favourite mountain, or with your beloved dog. Look closely and describe what you see, as much detail as you can, and then look again. What sort of expression do you have? Are you smiling, or grimacing? Are you relaxed or tense? What are you hiding? What sits just beneath the surface: worry, concern, boredom?

4. Now I want you to remember this time in your life, what came before the photo was taken and what came after? If you can't remember, think around it. If you can identify your age, you'll know where you were living, and make a guess at the key happenings in your life at that time; were you single, married? Recently divorced? If you are uncertain, still write it, but use the words 'perhaps' or 'maybe' – memoir is full of conjecture, as long as you are honest about what you don't know. When I think back to the key moment of seeing my father again after he had returned from India that I write about in the first chapter – and in my memoir – I do not remember anything that

happened around that key memory: how we got there, what we did afterwards. Did we leave with our dad, or make our own way home? Those were what Virginia Woolf calls non-moments, the everyday happenings of life, which do not stick in our memory. Yet imagining these happenings is how the narrative begins to grow.

5. If you are struggling, sit very still and close your eyes, or do some automatic writing to open the memory and get the words flowing. Alternatively, go on to the internet and look at YouTube videos of music from that period, or TV sitcoms, to remind you of the mood – but don't get sucked into the abyss!

6. Now you have material for a scene, inspired by a photograph. Write into it, see where it goes.

If you're keen and want further exercises:

7. Thinking back to Joan Didion's recollection that it snowed in August in Vermont, because to her summer was over, and my memory of Robin's big black coat, as a symbol of warmth and safety, I want you to recall an emotional moment and the images or objects that spring to mind in relation to it.

When you've written down these images or objects, think about what they symbolise – you might recall walking across a bridge, for instance, or taking a train ride – what is their greater meaning, and how does the greater meaning link with the themes you are interested in exploring? You can also make notes of why you remember certain objects over others.

Lastly, let's think about what we don't remember.

8. It might seem odd to have to create a concrete image from what you don't remember, but try to approach it another way. What if what is not remembered has a different kind of presence; it exerts a pull perhaps, and the question why? Maybe it comes in the form of a shadow, or a dark pervading presence. You know what might be there because you have been told, but for some reason it is wiped from your memory. We are all entitled to forget, of course – maybe the event didn't mean that much to you. But there is also repressed memory, from fear or shame, a kind of protective forgetting, which might be interesting to interrogate.

9. Set your timer for five minutes and write freely, starting with the sentence: 'I don't remember – but ...'

The self was
the God
image
within.

Individuaḥā.
Self - the central
of the personality -
the numinous connect
to the psyche
Individuaḥā - the
self presses -
there is an encounter
with the part of the
psyche - It happen
at middle age.
It really ser...

so me/they needs to
curve into the
world though
us.

NOTEM
WWW.NOTEM-STUDIO.COM

3

From the static into the moving world: the memoirisation of time

Recently I read Leslie Jamison's memoir, *Splinters: Another Kind of Love Story*, which follows her leaving her marriage with a one-year-old baby, driven by a need to live a more true and authentic life. Jamison has written many personal essays for the *New York Times*, and previous non-fiction, *The Empathy Exams* and *The Recovering*, but this she calls her first memoir. It circles around questions of self-transformation in life but also in writing. There is a passage where her friend tells her she has to pull away from their relationship, because she felt Leslie was always 'in the midst of some dramatic transformation … either poised on the threshold of some major change, or reeling in its aftermath'. From getting sober to drinking again to giving up booze for good; breaking up with a boyfriend to getting back together, marrying, having a baby, then getting a divorce. Leslie reflects on this: 'Maybe every rupture offered the chance to emerge as someone else, slightly altered, on the other side of each crisis.'

I found myself underlining so many passages in Jamison's memoir, because she gave me a language for what I too had felt within my marriage. I had married to correct an unhappy past, and didn't trust myself, and so opted for safe and normal. I had tried hard to 'show up' but it became increasingly difficult, and I couldn't shake off the feeling that I was living someone else's life. Eventually this left me in a state of wanting, searching for something – not better, but truer. But for years I sat tight. I could not leave. I could not break what I had painstakingly built; I could not cause pain to those I loved. Jamison refers to a teaching session where 'The students asked me impossibly earnest questions. Did I think authenticity required breaking an existing form or structure? I said, "Yes!" in a too-loud voice. I was talking about hybrid essays, and thinking about my divorce.' Yes! I muttered under my breath, because I knew – however destructive it was at the time – that truth wins in the end.

Does being a writer make me more provocative, more prone to nudging conventional structure, and, like Annie Ernaux, do I risk finding myself making 'a literary being of myself, someone who lives as if her experiences were to be written down someday'? Or am I a writer because I have an innate desire for self-improvement? Because I have the courage to confront personal and familial myths, whatever the consequences; to tolerate the discomfort of the in-between what was known and what might be, and to hold the tension of opposites? (And before you say it, this does not make me self-obsessed – what if the excavation of self is a kind of archaeology of the human spirit more generally, from the particular into the universals of pain, of grief and of love and loss? One must be honest with oneself, surely, not have half of the self hidden from view.)

Memoir is often driven by a quest to better understand events from the past, and as you learn more about yourself by revisiting those events, researching them, gaining distance from redrafting and crafting, and writing that new knowledge into the text, your perspective begins to shift and change, which then dictates the way the story is told. The life and the story become bound together like a double helix. Looking back to those difficult years of starting again beyond my marriage, I became more liberated and fearless because it had paid off to take the risk of listening to my heart, of doing 'the heart-work', as Rainer Maria Rilke encouraged the young poet in their exchange of letters. From the outside looking in, my life had become more difficult, but I was more myself than I had been in years. Enduring this and creating a new life helped me gain in courage and humility. Consequently, this fearlessness and willingness to go deeper into questions of need and desire made my writing more powerful.

In *Splinters*, Jamison asks whether perhaps it isn't what lies on the other side: is she more interested in the threshold-crossing itself? That liminal, in-between space, neither here nor yet other; standing on the edge with your arms outstretched, just before the jump, captivated still by the promise of change? As a teenager, she had always imagined heartbreak as bringing pleasure as well as pain, because it was 'ultimately provisional' – the necessary threshold to a deeper love on the horizon.

From a narrative point of view this is an interesting position from which to write. If I was to write about my marriage separation, I should place myself at a point of conflict. I take myself back to sitting in the garden alone, smoking a cigarette while my husband sits in the kitchen. He is in the warmth of inside, at the centre of all that we know, and I am on the periphery, and the sky is darkening. I remember how scared I felt in that transitory place, in the cold of outside, a place that I had chosen, but now I see its dramatic potential: I had a strong desire to leave, but I didn't want to wreck our lives. I both loved my husband and was not sure I could live with him. My dilemma is electric. I was on the cusp, from the static into the moving world.

The first words in *Splinters* are: 'The baby and I arrived at our sublet with garbage bags full of shampoo and teething crackers …'. Jamison and her 13-month-old daughter are literally in that liminal space, moving into a small dimly lit sublet right next to a fire station from which firemen strut about with chainsaws. The opening scenes capture the 'radical simultaneity' Jamison was experiencing at the time of her divorce, the dual experience of falling deeply in love with her daughter while her marriage was falling apart. She is caught between love and grief, with guilt thrown into the mix of wanting her working life back while venturing into single motherhood. Jamison struggles up the stairs to their new sublet, weighed down by garbage bags full of their past life, but also what they need to survive in the future. The stairs are the threshold between the old and the new. Great memoir contains the push and pull of attempted transformation, as does the therapist's treatment room, a liminal space between what was and what is to come. The old map is torn, no longer readable, and in this holding space a new map is drawn.

Speaking to the author Ali Millar about the experience of writing her debut memoir, *The Last Days*, about growing up in and away from the Jehovah's Witnesses cult, she writes about how, when working through trauma, 'memoir is poison and the cure. It's like you enter into a breach,' she says. 'I had this rupture and wasn't fully in the next life. I was in this in-between space. And the memoir offered me a way of stepping into the next life.' She also told me: 'When I left the religion, I went through a period of needing to be in a constant state of movement – a need to move forward, because I felt that if I was in flux, I was alright.' Writing her memoir helped her slow down and to look more intently at what she was escaping from. 'I didn't want to feel ashamed any more and I didn't want to conceal things. I was fed up with being stuck.'

To recapture the experience of sitting in the garden that day when my husband was in the kitchen, I must bring it alive with an immediacy that will make my reader have a visceral connection with the conflict I felt inside. I do this by engaging with symbol and sensory detail, entering the moment as if I were reliving it. I write about a garden chair upended on the lawn, and my fixation on the shadows between the slats on its back, made more prominent and given more contrast by the darkening light. But there is also a plastic toy gun on the lawn. *The cat steps from the house, walks past the gun, and sits at my feet.* The plastic toy gun belongs to the young children we have between us, but it also speaks of violence. The cat is perhaps the symbolic form of all that my husband and I are responsible for. That the cat walks past the gun and sits at my feet? Perhaps, if love transcends volatility, might it even be strengthened by it?

In writing this scene, I am also simultaneously aware of the retrospective position, looking back on the past with the hindsight of all I have come to know. It is a scene that is written in the present tense, but it holds the wisdom of insight in its selected detail and how hard those details work – they are what I call 'slanted detail' – that hold within them story and character, and even the yet-to-be-lived future that belongs to the moment, that the Lily of then has no idea of, despite the knowledge of the Lily of now. The wisdom exists in the subtext. *There are slats in the chair and they are widening, and the light of the kitchen is warm. I am outside. You are in the kitchen. I smoke the last of my cigarette.* I am both inside the moment and at one remove. The academic Celia Hunt coined a term for this contradictory state in creative writing, which is both deeply personal and moves away from the self, to become impersonal. She calls it 'reflexivity' and defines it in *Writing: Self and Reflexivity*, co-written with Fiona Sampson.

Reflexivity stems from reflection, but goes deeper, with the intention of reaching beyond contemplation to create something new. 'Reflexivity involves creating an internal space, distancing ourselves from ourselves, as it were, so that we are both "inside" and "outside" ourselves simul-taneously and able to switch back and forth fluidly and playfully from one position to the other, giving ourselves up to the experience of "self as other" whilst also retaining a grounding in our familiar sense of self.' This reflexive state allows a writer to engage with the specificity of their individual experience, 'imbuing the writing with felt life', while seeing it in the context of something greater, both the self and other, so that a work of art becomes 'a thing sufficient in itself'. Good memoir doesn't only capture what happened – that would be called anecdote

– it must also discover the greater significance of that happening, revealing hidden meaning and emotion, and how it relates to the larger landscape of loss, love, pain, renewal. Vivian Gornick calls this the situation and the story in her book of the same name. 'What happened to the writer is not what matters,' she writes. 'What matters is the larger sense that the writer is able to make of what happened.' We are of ourselves, but also of the world, after all. Writing memoir then becomes not only about story but also relationship: between the author, their experience and how it is transformed into story. If this is done with sufficient craft, your reader will also experience a transformation, of sorts. They will feel moved by what they read and might even see their own personal experience in a new and restorative light.

As Celia Hunt points out, reflexivity is innate in creative writing practice. It can't be forced. It comes with experience and developing a self-awareness of the writing process; not necessarily a self-consciousness, which can be debilitating, particularly when writing a first draft, but more the ability to move fluidly between these different positions, both personal and expansive. Reflexivity, writes Hunt, 'requires a kind of internal distancing, allowing a space to open up between ourselves and our material, so that it can develop a life of its own in our imagination.'

One such way of doing this is through what I think of as the 'memoirisation' of time, that is, the subtle dance between the two perspectives of 'then' and 'now'. On the one hand there is the memory of participation, of the concrete specifics in the moment of 'then' – the unmediated experience. Then there is the wide view, panning out to the reflective, broad sweeps and revelations of the retrospective position, from the point of view of 'now'. Gornick describes it as 'the situation' (the action from the past, or what we might call the plot: this happens, and then this happens, and then this), and 'the story', which is what the reflective voice of the 'now' makes of these events. In the 'now' the happenings are elevated from mere anecdote, given depth, in the attempt to answer the question, *Who cares?* In our daily lives, we get caught up in any given moment, swept up in the emotion, whether it be losing our rag or a rush of affection, and it is only with hindsight that we can revisit these scenes and begin to understand what else was going on: old patterns triggered; the repetitive (and often unhelpful!) undercurrent between two lovers; the point of view of the other person in the room – Barbara Hepworth's 'perfect balance between the conscious and unconscious life', the material and intuition. As I demonstrated in the garden scene above, when writing memoir this double perspective is always present, whether explicitly or implicitly.

The writer and critic Phillip Lopate writes of how the dual perspective allows the reader to 'participate vicariously in the experience as if it were lived (the child's confusions and misapprehensions, say), while benefitting from the sophisticated wisdom of the adult perspective'; while the memoirist Sue Silverman calls the memoirisation of time the 'voice of innocence' and the 'voice of wisdom'. The lived experience brings the text alive, but the more mature point of view is essential to memoir because it is a more dispassionate view, with the benefit of hindsight and all the narrator has come to know. The 'voice of wisdom' interprets events from the past, reaching towards some new insight and meaning. Readers are not so much interested in the raw, unmediated emotion of any given moment, they want to feel the deeper significance of that moment and they want to learn something. This involves the writer viewing events from two vantage points, then and now, and the skilled memoirist learns to move between these two states seamlessly and reflexively, and to use that movement to their advantage.

This is demonstrated with great skill by the essayist Scott Russell Sanders in his essay 'Under the Influence', which is about the enduring and toxic legacy of his father's alcoholism. In this essay, Sanders is both the damaged child and the man, himself also a father, trying to understand *and* stand apart from that influence, despite also knowing he will never be wholly free of it. It is right, then, that throughout his essay Sanders switches and sometimes even merges the two perspectives, always at the mercy of alcoholism's insidious threat. He establishes this early by immediately orientating the reader in both the 'then' of childhood and the 'now' of himself as storyteller:

> My father drank ... I use the past tense not because he never quit drinking but because he quit living. That is how the story ends for my father ... The story continues for my brother, my sister, my mother and me, and will continue as long as memory holds.

He not only jumps through time and back again, but he draws attention to those jumps, making clear his role as the writer telling his story, now, at his keyboard, with the wisdom of maturity and hindsight. He does this by writing about the writing technique itself ('I use the past tense', as you see in the quote above), but also in the following paragraph: 'In the perennial present of memory,

I slip into the garage or barn …'. This slipping into present tense when writing about memory is common in memoir, and often comes from an instinctive place. Particularly traumatic and difficult memory returns to us as if it were happening once more, and the present tense brings it alive on the page.

In these early passages, Sanders also condenses time: 'to see my father tipping back the flat green bottles of wine, the brown cylinders of whiskey, the cans of beer disguised in paper bags … he stashes the bottle or can inside his jacket, under the workbench, between two bales of hay, and we both pretend the moment has not occurred'. This shows the awful, repetitive nature of his dad's illness, that it is a specific moment but it is equally any number of moments blurred into one. The situation might be different, but the story is the same: his father's drinking and his father's denial, and the child's complicity in that denial, as happens in millions of families across the world.

In his memoir *The Day That Went Missing*, Richard Beard writes about his brother's drowning, similarly drawing attention to the writing itself in his exploration of memory and denial. In the opener he sets the scene of his family on holiday in Cornwall in 1978.

> The family is Mum, Dad and four boys. I am second in a declension that goes 13, 11, 9, 6. My brother Nicholas Beard is nine. For nearly forty years I haven't said his name, but in writing I immediately slip into the present tense, as if he's here, he's back. Writing can bring him to life.

Throughout the memoir, Beard collects evidence to support his understanding of events as they happened, in contrast to what had been claimed by his family. He – like Sanders – still struggles with the child within him and his own inability to truly face his complex feelings of pain and guilt around his brother's drowning, and we see this explicitly worked out on the page. Every time Beard attempts to return to the site of the drowning, it eludes him: he gets lost, or he cannot remember the name of the beach because he has left it in a notebook in the back of a car he does not have access to; or he visits at the wrong time of day and the weather or tide obscures. When Beard finally makes it to the beach, the past and present collide as one, completely overwhelming him, like a rushing tide: he is both himself as a man and an 11-year-old child, both the boy anticipating fun and a week later pretending nothing has changed. He is his mother holding a size three shoe, and he is under the skin of his dad – all the time waiting for the pain to really hit him as an adult, to give the event the significance it deserves.

Before Beard wrote *The Day That Went Missing*, he wrote fiction, but the ghost of his brother kept appearing. Beard tells me: 'In the novel *Lazarus Is Dead* I invented a younger brother for the biblical character Lazarus. I called him Amos, and I drowned him in a made-up version of Lake Galilee, I suspect to try and kill the memory.' Beard was still caught up in the denial that had smothered his family around his brother's death. But, as Beard goes on to say, his ploy failed. Instead, it only highlighted the denial. 'I expected a reaction from my family: for the first time, one of my books contained a public retelling of our true life-changing event,' Beard says. But there was no reaction. Beard himself had crossed a line, but only just, because his family would not – could not – yet follow. He was balancing on the threshold between denial and beginning to face the truth, one foot on and one foot off.

In the end he chose truth, and the more direct form that is memoir, to begin to unravel what had happened with hard evidence and to make the facts undeniable: that he was in the water with his brother when his brother drowned. He went back to the area in Cornwall where they holidayed and retraced his steps; he spoke to the coastguards who found his brother. He spoke to his mother, pushing her into dangerous territory in his insistence that she face the truth.

> Nearly four decades after the event, I have carried out my version of an inquest. I've tried to stop time in Cornwall on a single day, though I've never before worked like this, surrounded by the debris of the past. I navigate a floor covered in photos and school reports, letters and random items of vintage clothing. I sit down, I stand up, I welcome and curse the return of feeling and kick my chair across the room. Feel, damn you, feel something or forget, forget it ever happened.

The reason he kept going back was because, in his own words: 'This event was powerful in my sense of self, and therefore I thought it would be powerful in a novel, but somehow it transcended that – the reality of it became more important. There was a real-life implication that was worth following through.' The memoir then became a conduit for the truth, not felt just by Beard but also eventually by his family.

Similarly, throughout Sanders's essay 'Under the Influence', we have clues as to why the story is so important to the author's emotional development. Quite early on, he reflects,

> I am only trying to understand the corrosive mixture of helplessness, responsibility, and shame that I learned to feel as the son of an alcoholic. I realize now that I did not cause my father's illness, nor could I have cured it. Yet for all this

grownup knowledge, I am still ten years old, my own son's age, and as that boy I struggle in guilt and confusion to save my father from pain.

Like Beard, he is both the child and the adult with the wisdom of how he still carries that child inside him. Both free of the past and caught still in its briars. A child of an alcoholic, always under the influence.

But as the essay progresses, we see that Sanders now has a responsibility for the next generation, his own son, who himself takes to heart his father's sadness. 'I write, therefore, to drag into the light what eats at me – the fear, the guilt, the shame – so that my own children may be spared.' For his son's sake, he takes the risky step of facing that fear, and putting a stop to the cycle of pain. The reflective passages in 'Under the Influence' are the essay's soul; they are what grip the reader and bring tears to the eyes. They are points of revelation for the author and therefore become a gift of revelation to us. Sanders's mastering of craft allows a different perspective to come into being.

In the prologue of my memoir, I too play with the memoirisation of time. I stand in a particular place in a generic present day, in a new home, with Robin, attempting to finally find peace after the disruption of my marriage separation. But there is one last thread that needs knotting. Seven years after my father's death I am still haunted by him; still living the legacy of our complicated love in my grieving of a marriage that was doomed from the start. I am still on a threshold, but I am also on my way home. A phone call with my brother is the trigger for change – for me to step back out into the moving world and finally let my father go.

From a technical perspective, my position in the present day allows me to dance between different events from my past: not just my father's funeral, but also the day I imagine he clicked on the email that was to be his downfall. Also, my own painful grief and how it manifested itself in drinking and resisting going home to my children, or participating fully in the life my husband and I had built. These were all scenes that I had laboured on individually – my 'moments', as we explored in the first chapter. They were memories of significance, which initially I wrote up as individual scenes full of heat and pain and unmediated chaos, before I found that voice of guiding wisdom, my golden arrow, to help direct the way. I will write more about this voice in the chapter, 'The holder of the threads', but here it is worth noting that the prologue was the last chapter that I wrote.

By the time I wrote the prologue, I had found my dispassionate narrator – what Vivian Gornick calls the persona, 'the instrument of illumination' – but I also had to retain the power of the unmediated feeling self from those early scenes I had written, in order to capture the hold that my father had had over me many years before. That longing is what Celia Hunt describes as the most personal part, the most primal painful and disappointed love that a daughter feels for her charismatic but absent father. After I had reached the end of the memoir and a natural sense of resolution, I had to identify the emotional trajectory of the story, and craft it accordingly, retaining the heat, confusion and pain of the early chapters combined with a slow unravelling, before finding cohesion again.

Similarly, when writing *The Day That Went Missing*, Beard had to rely on his skills of storytelling to bring home the extraordinary journey of discovery as it had happened. 'Writing this book changed me as a writer as well as a person. The process of finding out about the past was a genuine process of discovery. I genuinely didn't know the date that my brother had died, and I didn't know his birthday. It also led to a clear denouement to go back to that place and try to relive it, and it was a surprise to me what happened there, so the experience and the writing came together.' He spoke of the importance of retaining the genuine sense of mystery when it comes to editing: 'it does help if you are a bit stupider than in real life. You might find things out, but you don't immediately understand them. This is a way of characterising yourself in memoir.'

As we saw in the introductory chapter 'From repatterning to becoming', Beard is explicit about how being a writer has helped him come to terms with the trauma of his brother's drowning. Embarking on his memoir, he was committed to facing the truth, to write the best book he could; but also honouring the past by going deeper in his understanding. 'If I had gone through this process of revisiting where the family tragedy happened, not writing about it, and not knowing what to do with it, I think it would have been more disturbing. But I knew what I wanted to do with it, which was to make it as honest an expression as possible of what was happening, and that was its own support,' he tells me. It is almost as if the memoir becomes his insulation; it helps him reach beyond his own personal reasons for going back. Writing is generative, after all. He goes on to say it was 'almost a written version of therapy. Almost like doing therapy with yourself.'

The experience of writing my memoir about my father was very much like this. In *Moments of Being*, Virginia Woolf writes of how she was obsessed with her mother, from her premature death when Virginia was 13 to the age of 44, when one day, while walking, she 'made up' her semi-autobiographical novel, *To the Lighthouse*, 'in a great, apparently involuntary rush'. And I can see a similar obsession on my part with my father. He was under my skin, in my heart, pulling on me, dragging me back. I was caught in his web; the grip of him when I got married and the shocking experience of witnessing his death to alcoholism was further isolating, driving a wedge between me and my husband. But through the experience of writing my memoir about him and his influence on my life, something changed.

On that walk that Woolf took, the narrative of *To the Lighthouse* came to her like 'blowing bubbles out of a pipe – one idea bursting from the other'. She wrote the book very quickly and, once it was complete, her mother ceased to haunt her: 'I no longer hear her voice; I do not see her …'. After my father died, I dreamed of him, saw his figure in bulky men with luxurious hair, his ghost in the streets of Primrose Hill where I wished he might have settled and grown old. But through the various stages of writing *Sins of My Father* – from that first cathartic rush, a kind of purging in the first draft, to reflection, finding and crafting story, redrafting, further research and editing – I moved through various stages of distance, nurturing an ability to both absorb myself in and objectify the experience. I realised this process could be both artful and therapeutic at the same time.

While studying for my PhD, I discovered the word 'transliminal' in relation to the personal narrative. I first read it in Margot Singer and Nicole Walker's edited collection *Bending Genre*, where Lawrence Sutin describes it as 'cross-genre explorations' – which artists and writers have been experimenting with for all time. He cites William Blake, whose masterpiece *The Marriage of Heaven and Hell* brought together engravings, poetry and prose; and Dante in *La Vita Nuova*, merging poetry, memoir and criticism. But Sutin also brings this term closer to lived experience, referring to the daily state of:

> Everyday crossings that everyone makes from sleeping to waking, private to public, culture to culture, talking to listening, paper to screen, paying attention to not, sobriety to excess to silence, history to fantasy to memory to dream, all the while in and out of love and hate and certainty and utter incomprehension.

I love this description as it reminds me of how in flux we always are, despite our desire to try to pin ourselves down with definitions, diagnoses, decisions; despite our restlessness and impatience to be at a certain destination before we could possibly arrive.

Sutin describes transliminal as generating 'a roaming personal consciousness of the author as a means of more deeply exploring the subject in question'. This might involve drawing upon a range of ideas, theories and criticism to add layers to the narrative, then showing the workings out on the page; an author like a magpie attracted to what shines. The author Susanna Crossman does this brilliantly in her memoir *Home Is Where We Start* and spoke eloquently to me on the subject: 'My life only interests me as material for approaching the human experience, exploring questions.' She compares this to what Goethe calls 'delicate empiricism', 'a mixture of imagination, intuition, and facts'.

I also find that my reading around a subject, whether it is poetry, fiction, philosophy, or psychology, supports my thinking and enriches my understanding. It seems natural then that some of that reading is threaded through the text, making a collage of what is recalled, what is imagined and what is learned. This broadens the discussion, and helps in one's quest to find meaning. By recording the conversations an author has with their reading, they show their 'thinking on the page' as Phillip Lopate describes it in *To Show and to Tell*. This gives the text an intimacy that draws in the reader. The reader trusts you, and you take their hand. Moving into other writers' thoughts and theories can also act as a protection, a diversion from the more personal material (I go more deeply into this in the next chapter, 'Radical deconstruction').

Because by writing about my father I came to understand him better than I had when he was alive, his ghost faded at every turn, until, when the book was published, he finally disappeared. I felt a rush of pain when I saw the cover of the hardback book, that sweet photograph of me on his hip taken on the doorstep of my grandparents' house on my aunt and uncle's wedding day – such a personal photograph of a family celebration – and I wondered if I had made a terrible mistake. Seeing my father's face next to the word *Sin* – a word I had put there. How had I done this to him? He was dead and could not defend himself. But I let myself feel that pain, that guilt, whatever you might call it, and I let it go. I had written the book, but it was no longer just my story. By my redrafting, editing, refining and crafting, the story was unfurling its wings and getting ready to fly. It now belonged in the world, and I was ready for it to metamorphose into something that no longer belonged to me.

Now as I write this, nearly two years after my memoir was published, I have no real sense of my father at all. As Woolf said about writing *To the Lighthouse*, 'I did for myself what psycho-analysts do for their patients. I expressed some very long felt and deeply felt emotion. And in expressing it I explained it and then laid it to rest.'

I wonder now if writing is a type of mourning, what the author Louise DeSalvo, names 'symbolic repair' in *Writing as a Way of Healing*. In the examples listed above, it certainly complements, and even – in the case of Beard – kick starts the grieving process. Does the book then become a kind of memorial to a lost person, or a lost part of the self (or maybe both)? 'By writing about them,' writes DeSalvo, 'we give them posthumous life.' Damian Barr in his memoir *Maggie & Me* brought to life a friend who had died: '[Mark] has a sort of life that he doesn't have literally any more. People know him,' Barr said.

So often art is made from wounds, a way of generating something good and profound from negative experience. DeSalvo writes of how writing became survival for the author Isabel Allende when her daughter was in a coma, how Allende's agent visited her at her daughter's bedside and urged her 'to write a letter to Paula', instead of suffering wordlessly. Allende does just this: 'I plunge into these pages in an irrational attempt to overcome my terror ...', and as DeSalvo tells us, Allende's daughter's illness propelled her mother to understand her own life differently. 'You Paula', Allende writes, 'have given me this silence in which to examine my path through the world.' She was able to return to parts of her past she had previously believed to have 'little meaning' and see the patterns of loss that had haunted her. Allende could not save her daughter, 'but giving form to her pain allowed Allende to feel her despair, allowed her to connect it to the events in her life that occasioned it, even as it kept her despondency manageable,' writes DeSalvo. Powerless in the wake of her daughter's death, Allende saved herself. DeSalvo quotes Allende stating that she could take her own life, or 'write a book that would heal me ... I went on writing because I could not stop.' Through her writing she was able to integrate the horror of losing her child into her life.

Is it possible to therapise ourselves through writing? From loss to growth, finding order from chaos? Beard's *The Day That Went Missing* is evidence of his and his mother's journey from denial to acknowledgement; *Splinters* is the artful result of Jamison's restlessness to rediscover herself outside of her marriage and create a life as a single working mother. DeSalvo tells us how Allende calls her writing 'therapy', and how she works through the pain of living not by speaking to a therapist, but through writing.

The most obvious difference between writing and therapy is that writing is solitary, whereas therapy relies on the relationship between 'patient' and therapist. But both practices are concerned with the human experience, and more broadly the human condition and the active development of the self. Both use language as their tool, despite one being in written form, the other oral. And both rely on dialogue. The analysand learns to speak freely with their analyst, whereas, as Woolf said of writing *To the Lighthouse*, the writer learns to hone a dialogue with themselves. This dialogue is between the different parts of the self, but also with regard to ethical parameters – what you can and cannot write about in terms of your own emotional safety and that of those you love.

The therapeutic relationship is often driven by a need for change in the form of a desire in the analysand for a guiding hand to help them step over the threshold. Like writing, therapy can help give form to the abstracts of feeling and emotion so they can be articulated and understood. As Arabella Kurtz says to J. M. Coetzee in *The Good Story*, 'In the consulting room we see people who communicate things about themselves, often unconsciously, which are at odds with the story they consciously tell.'

This reminds me very much of the mentoring relation-ship. 'I am not a therapist' is undoubtedly the first thing I say in a new relationship with a mentee, but the mentor role does involve a lot of reading between the lines, and helping a writer find their true story: the one that matters most to them. This can often be withheld, either con-sciously or unconsciously, because the content is too difficult, or the writer has not yet reached a level of self-understanding (or might even be deceiving themselves). Or the writer might have chosen to write about something entirely different, when they are haunted by the ghosts of the thing they are trying to avoid. A literary mentor's role, like a therapist, is to create a safe holding space, for the writer to step out of their comfort zone and go deeper and sit longer with difficult emotion. 'One way of thinking about psychoanalysis is to say that it is aimed at setting free the narrative or autobiographical imagination,' says Kurtz. As a teacher and mentor, I do much the same. Also, like a therapist, a mentor acts as a mirror to the writer, reflecting what they say, and helping them untangle difficult feelings around experience, but also to help them find meaning in events from the past. This helps a writer objectify their experience, to view it from outside, which is the first step towards healing, but also towards having a readership.

As a mentor and teacher of memoir, much of my work goes into building trust and giving space to what can take many years. As well as helping to free the narrator's voice and their imagination, a mentor encourages a writer to reach into the depths of their version of events, to help them find their own specific truth and to build in confidence enough to take risks. Sometimes this involves simply drawing their attention to the absences in the text, where they are not prepared to go, to give the writer a chance to talk through their concerns. It might also involve a certain amount of gentle probing to help the writer get to the heart of what really matters to them.

Recently I worked with someone who had waited until her parents had died to write her version of events, and I wanted her to go more deeply into certain memories, to write them as she had lived them so the reader could stand at her side and experience it as closely as if they were standing alongside her as a child. This writer had felt ashamed of what had happened to her and was expecting her readers to judge her as harshly as her parents had. The result was that her writing was summative and weighted heavily towards exposition – the reflective, knowing voice of hindsight – rather than letting the story emerge in felt past experience. Her reticence and fear were letting her down. There is a certain contract we must have with ourselves if we are to call ourselves writers, and that is to respect that role and do it to the best we can. But we also owe it to ourselves to be true to our experience and bring that experience alive so it can speak for itself.

It is worth noting here one key difference between the therapeutic relationship and the relationship a writer has with themselves and the page – and this is the challenge of the private becoming public, and the fear of exposure when a memoir is published (this will be the focus of the next chapter and Chapter 6.) Despite this, the first draft of a memoir should evolve from a freedom similar to that felt within the therapeutic room, because self-censorship kills creativity and the deep connection needed to touch the sensory nerve of subjective truth. You'll have plenty of time to reflect and redraft, to talk to family members and think through what should be deleted and what should remain, and what might be disguised through writing technique and metaphor.

Try this:

1. I want you to place yourself in a present-day moment – when I say present, it doesn't need to be today or yesterday (it can be ten years ago), but there must be a reason why you chose it. Is it a defining 'moment', as we saw in Chapter 1, or perhaps an inciting incident when everything is on an axis, everything is about to change?

The moment you choose must allow for reflection, for asking yourself a question. The one I am choosing here is a moment I sat in the dining room of the home I lived in with my husband and two children, and I am on the phone to schools in the city I am planning to move to. I had never really lived out of London – not beyond being at university – and here I was, considering a total relocation. I had to find somewhere to live, find new schools, reinvent myself and my children's lives in a whole new place, with nothing that was familiar, no friends, not the community we took for granted. I choose this moment, because it stays with me.

2. In my imagination it comes to me as a dark and shadowy image. There was dark wood around me – in the table I sat at, the wooden floorboards beneath my feet – but the room appears dark as well. The only light was from the green of the garden and its neighbouring trees. I was scared. I had a little notebook that I had dedicated all my findings to, dates of when I had to do school applications by, the schools I had phoned, the open days, the ones that were over-subscribed and others that had places. But also, from here, I can look back and ask: *Why? How did we get here?*

3. I can jump to the day when the estate agent came to the house and told me how much she loved it, how lucky we were, and I cried because I didn't want to leave. I can jump forward still to the mammoth move a year or so later, piles of boxes, dust, all our belongings stuffed into the attic. The day my daughter came down to me in the sunshine, and the house looked so beautiful, and she was crying because the window was open in her

room and the birds were singing, the neighbourhood children outside, and she did not want to leave. Or I can go back in time from this moment, to when I first saw that house, back when it was on the market, and set my heart on it, and drove round and round the block to take in the area and the neighbourhood, how my daughter, then just a baby, slept in a baby seat in the back. And I couldn't believe I was here – considering buying a grown-up house. That it felt as if I had landed.

4. And time opens up, memory leads to memory leads to memory. So many memories from this time are from inside my car. It was a place where I could get some respite because the children would be quiet, or often slept, and it was the only time I listened to music. And now I jump forward great strides to my teenage daughter playing the music I played back then in the car, the songs that defined my emotional state at the time. And how she calls her playlist Nostalgia, and on it is a photograph of me and her from a family holiday when I was still married and still with my children's dad in Greece. She has her arm around me, and she is leaning up against me, and I am studying the ground. I look incredibly sad. This is how I see it because I know what is to come. I'm not sure she sees it like that. I wonder if she simply sees a mother and a daughter, both dressed in white and both tanned, arms entwined on a family holiday together in Greece.

5. Now I want you to choose a still point – a static point – that holds the weight of story, and see how it helps you take your first steps into the moving world.

Just one more thing:

Go out and find yourself a notebook and call it your quote book, and carry it around with you always. You can write down bits of poems, or quotes from articles you have read, thoughts or things that matter, however random they might be.

I feel gutted, nervous, sick, anxious
and don't know why. You are sitting
across the room on your guitar in your
usual serious and passionate way. I love you
I want to hold you. I want everyone in this
room to disappear. I want to cuddle
you but I can't because of fear. I am
scared because I want this to last.

4

Radical deconstruction: embodied writing and protective forms

Since publishing *Sins of My Father*, I have been skirting around a new idea, trying to make it dance – but it's missing an arm and a leg, and appears lopsided. I know I am avoiding the deeply personal stuff, because when I engage with it the writing comes alive. But I am not sure I want to go there. Why? I fear that writing through the taboo of a woman leaving a perfectly good marriage and hurting her children will expose me and hurt those I love. I could write it as fiction, of course, or as autofiction, which sits in that space in-between, taking inspiration from life but moving beyond transparent leaps of the imagination and speculation. But to me the word 'fiction' denotes fabrication; I do not want my shame to prevent me from telling it as it is. What I teach my students is that there is another way, in fact multiple ways, of protecting yourself when working with flammable material. It involves going deeper, going through rather than over, to an intimate engagement with one's subject. In this way I can transcend the literal description of a mother unhappily married and forging ahead to create a new life.

If I write into the conundrum itself, I land on symbol: a broken vessel, shards placed back together but in a different configuration, but the edges aren't jagged and ugly, the glue tacky and dirty. Rather, it is a kintsugi bowl, beautiful *because* of its fractures, its fault part of its design. The broken shapes are connected by not just any glue, but with gold. The philosophy of *wabi sabi* – the Japanese aesthetic that sees beauty in imperfection – might then become a theme, a recurring motif throughout, or it might even dictate form. I could write in fragments, metaphorically speaking, into the breakage – or both. Think back to Noreen Masud's *A Flat Place*, in which finding flat landscapes becomes the drive of the entire book; or what about Carmen Maria Machado's *In the Dream House*, which uses the repeat metaphor of a 'dream house' to describe a psychic state, but also a literal place of abuse and coercive control?

In these memoirs and many more besides, the form protects the difficult content – whether it be Complex Post-Traumatic Stress Disorder, or violence within a relationship. Because of this framework, this 'scaffolding' as Clare Best calls it, authors can free themselves within the form's walls. In a recent workshop I attended on hybrid forms, the writer Tania Hershman called this 'liberation through constraint' – by knowing where the boundaries are, a writer has more confidence to experiment and play. The content shapes the form, and the form works hard for the story, both as a framing device and as a way of revealing meaning, slowly, sometimes obliquely, with originality and nuance. Writing like this can be deeply personal and rooted in the self of the individual writer.

You might want to write from within a traumatic experience. It might be a minority story, or an abuse story, or a story of illness, or dissociation or disembodiment, which has been colonised or silenced by cultural and familial norms about suffering. It might be a story that mainstream culture has failed to even imagine, as in the case of *In the Dream House* and its exploration of lesbian domestic abuse, because, as Machado tells us, 'our culture does not have an investment in helping queer folks understand what their experiences *mean*.' In *The Limits of Autobiography: Trauma and Testimony*, the American academic Leigh Gilmore writes of how trauma, which stems from the Greek word meaning 'wound', 'refers to the self-altering, even self-shattering experience of violence, injury and harm ... that trauma is beyond language ... that language fails in the face of trauma and trauma mocks language with its insufficiency'. Through her writing, Machado attempts to discover a personalised language and symbol for queer domestic abuse, and interrogates and challenges the culture invested in its silencing. By doing this, she finds concrete form for the unnameable, and invites the reader into the experience. A body finds its own language. A body speaks. After all, as Susan Sontag famously wrote in *Illness as Metaphor* and *AIDS and Its Metaphors*, 'Everyone who is born holds dual citizenship, in the kingdom of the well and in the kingdom of the sick'. We will all be affected by illness and trauma at some point.

Memoir is fertile ground for this kind of embodied writing, from *within* rather than *about* an experience of trauma or illness. It is a way of writing *into* what might otherwise be wordless or unspeakable, finding expression for what it is like to be caught in the centre, or in the undertow, of an emotion or physical experience. It gives shape and expression to what otherwise feels disembodied or dissociative. The effect on a reader is more emotional and visceral and involving than if they were simply reading a blow-by-blow account of an experience. According to Arthur W. Frank in *The Wounded Storyteller*, his part-memoir, part-ode to narrative medicine, 'The illness *story* begins in wreckage, having lost its map and destination. The *story* is both interrupted and it is about interruption. In the illness stories what begins as the breakdown of narrative-life's interruption by illness is transformed into *another kind* of narrative.' Frank goes on to demonstrate this point by writing of a popular band repeatedly playing the time signature wrong, but so consistently that it became their own time signature. Sinéad Gleeson writes in her essay collection *Constellations* on the effects of growing up with arthritis and later suffering from a rare form of leukaemia: 'The sick body has its own narrative impulse.'

Almost a decade after Virginia Woolf's ground-breaking short essay 'On Being Ill' was published, it continues – maybe now more than ever – to help writers in their quest to find a language to express their own unique illness experience. Woolf writes of the intense and sensory nature of illness, and how it can enhance language; that through its prism, language becomes more carnal, more immediate: 'In illness words seem to possess a mystic quality … In health … our intelligence domineers over our senses. But in illness, with the police off duty, we creep beneath some obscure poem by Mallarmé or Donne, some phrase in

Latin or Greek, and the words give out their scent, and ripple like leaves.' The words of illness are 'more primitive', she writes, 'more sensual, more obscene'. More insistent perhaps. No wonder, when 'all day and all night the body intervenes'. But despite this, she writes, there is no place for the body in literature, which is concerned only with the mind.

> People write always about the doings of the mind; the thoughts that come to it; its noble plans; how it has civilised the universe. They show it ignoring the body in the philosopher's turret; or kicking the body, like an old leather football, across leagues of snow and desert in the pursuit of conquest or discovery.

In her excellent *Paris Review* essay 'More Primitive, More Sensual, More Obscene', the author Marina Benjamin references how much reading Woolf's 'On Being Ill' helped in her own understanding of the immediate, shocking and carnal experience of being thrown into a premature menopause after having an hysterectomy. But she also confesses that she discovered Woolf's essay late, after she had written her memoir, *Middlepause*, on the same subject, 'I wrote it as I lived it – as an embodied woman, come into the inheritance of aging.' Following her operation, Benjamin had been thrown into a state of physical and emotional shock, wandering around the world 'queasily off-balance. Out and about on basic errands in my neighbourhood, I'd be so high on a sense of unreality as to be practically levitating.' Her speech was affected, too. 'Words flew from my brain and dissipated upwards like a flock of birds. Nouns, in particular, kept disappearing.' She found it difficult to find the right words for everyday things, like toaster, iron and kettle; she was stripped of language, and her altered body demanded a new kind of attention.

In her essay, Benjamin reflects on how the experience put her in touch with what Virginia Woolf describes as 'the daily drama of the body'. The shock of the physical changes in her demanded that she notice.

> Menopause asked that I pay closer attention to bodily experience almost minute by minute, because with each bodily dip and lurch, each hormonal spike and roundabout, every shiver and sweat that wrenched my guts, a new filter was placed between my reality and that of the larger world.

Woolf's essay helped Benjamin by giving her a language to describe her isolation and estrangement. For Woolf, when ill, 'the whole language of life lies remote and fair, like the shore seen from a ship far out at sea'. This 'language of life' becomes alien to someone confined to their sickbed. Benjamin writes: 'No wonder Woolf called for a new language … for describing where we speak from when we find ourselves in this altered state.' Benjamin reflects that in illness 'meaning comes to us sensually first' and that the ill must 'speculate carnally'. In her attempt to meet and understand that pain, the change in her body and the consequent shift in her consciousness and relationship with herself, Benjamin uses the term 'my minded body' as if placing her mind where it had not previously been. She writes of how finally this disruption in her life forced her to realign herself, and how this had a positive effect on her writing – it helped her to be more herself, more authentic, rather than 'channelling', a type of 'posturing', even 'ventriloquism', trying to impress the 'intellectual giants', mostly men. Benjamin discovers that writing from within her body is an act of radical feminism. 'In pain or grief, love, rage, or illness, in hormonal extremes or sleepless desperation,' Benjamin writes, 'the body gifts us a window onto the world that changes what we see by virtue of shifting how we see it.'

The author and poet Polly Atkin starts her memoir, *Some of Us Just Fall*, with a kind of mission statement of her intention for the memoir to reflect the experience of living inside a body that is burdened by various chronic health conditions (Ehlers-Danlos syndrome and haemochromatosis). Atkin takes Woolf's essay 'On Being Ill' to another level, understanding Woolf's 'undiscovered countries' of illness as part of an otherworld: 'like a dreamscape'. Atkin writes, 'these strange countries are not merely observed, but felt. We do not just become aware of our own mortality in illness.' She quotes Woolf writing about the sensation of 'going down into the pit of death' and feeling the 'waters of annihilation close above our heads'. She continues by writing that the features of the landscape are simultaneously external, and internal: 'They are not the seemingly inert things of the well and waking world.'

But, like Benjamin, Atkin does not see this as a negative experience. When we spoke, I was moved by her reflection that the 'illness place can be transportative, not restrictive. It is not a cave, but a corridor, a passage through'. In her memoir, Atkin describes how, when she is unwell, she moves more into her body, and that her body is a wilderness of an expanding universe and of possibilities. Writing becomes a way of achieving sovereignty over one's own experience, and when that writing is shared through history, over generations, it reaches out to the struggling and vulnerable, still stranded on their own 'shore seen from a ship far out at sea', to join hands.

When we think of conventional narrative, we think of something linear that moves steadily towards an end point. It might have a few peaks and bumps along the way, but it will generally come to some kind of closure or satisfying resolution: a neat and tidy ending. For many who are living with trauma or illness, and particularly chronic illness, recovery is not an option. It is more common that a life is interrupted by pain and medical intervention, illness following periods of wellness, relapse. Growing up, Atkin was prone to bone breakages, had joints that easily dislocated, was troubled by fatigue. 'How do you tell a story to someone else when you can't understand it yourself as something with a beginning, a middle and an end, but only as an assembly of interwoven episodes? Of fracture after fracture.' She goes on to write that the chronically ill life is lived as repetition and variance, and that the only way she can write her memoir is through fragments – which she does – because 'it's the only way I know how to tell this story with any honesty'.

Writing in fragments is natural for a writer like Atkin, who has a poetry background, but who also turned to poetry because of the practical nature of its short and condensed form at a time in her teens when she was so unwell that she didn't have the attention span for writing anything longer. But the fragmentary nature also reflects the way Atkin and many other disabled people feel in their everyday life: 'I was so used to being outside the narrative; the octopus, not the human ... Physically, bodily dislocated, socially dislocated, dehumanised.' By writing into the dislocation, Atkin reclaims the interruptions in her life as hers to tell. Talking to me about her own struggles, Atkin shared a profound realisation: that rather than having a beginning, middle and end, she had discovered, against the odds, the 'grace of continuation' – the beauty and joy of continuing life.

Despite always knowing something was amiss, Atkin didn't receive a proper diagnosis until she was in her thirties. Her years of living undiagnosed or misdiagnosed were dark, when she was victim to what she describes as 'gaslighting' from doctors who didn't believe her when she spoke of her symptoms. Atkin writes a lot about the implicit power of the doctor and the comparative voicelessness of the patient; Atkin's situation made worse by sexism, when the (male) doctor refuses to listen to the (female) nurse and her mother, who are both convinced Atkin has broken her leg. The 'gaslighting' Atkin refers to will be familiar to many chronically ill and disabled people, simply because so often the illness or disabled story disrupts the usual wellness narrative and can feel uncomfortable for many.

Jenn Ashworth told me that when she was writing *Notes Made While Falling*, about her experience of living through severe physical, mental and emotional agony in the aftermath of haemorrhaging during the labour of her second child, 'I was really aware of the type of stories that sick people are supposed to write – the recovery memoirs, the good news stories, the "look at the mess in the rear view mirror" type tales. I didn't have that type of story available to me – I was writing from inside the experience – and I started to wonder if the idea of "recovery memoir" was actually a way of making sure the still-sick person didn't speak.' But Frank reminds us:

'[the illness stories'] uncomfortable quality is all the more reason they have to be told. Otherwise, the interrupted voice remains silenced.'

In *The Wounded Storyteller* Frank writes of how doctors have traditionally 'colonised' the illness experience by speaking for their patients, rather than listening closely to the particulars of their symptoms. This imposition of their views and beliefs upon the patient's experience amounts to a kind of 'medical colonisation'. Frank compares the necessary reclamation of language, which we see in essays like Woolf's and Benjamin's, and the illness story, to post-colonialism – 'the demand to speak rather than be spoken for and to represent oneself rather than being represented or, in the worst cases, rather than being effaced entirely'. Personal narrative then becomes a platform to discover a voice that has been subsumed, and a way to exert oneself, to feel empowered.

The writer Jacqueline Alnes explores the dichotomy of the doctor/patient relationship in her essay 'What Remains' about living with a disorientating neurological illness, which includes bouts of memory loss. At the start of the essay, she presents herself as a 20-year-old in a hotel room, soon after returning from a study trip to Peru where she had one of the first of her neurological episodes. She writes this section in the third person, which gives the reader a stronger sense of Alnes's dissociation from herself, both in the moment of the neurological episode, and also looking back at herself in the hotel bed.

> The girl's mother kneels by the bed. 'Do you want to go for a short walk?' Formerly muscular from running, the girl's limbs are a spectre of their old strength. The girl looks up, eyes glassy, and nods. Her mother's hand supporting her back,

she eases a leg from the mattress. Without warning, her head begins to rock from side to side on its own. Within her skull, the sensation of mist enveloping a mountain, everything clouded. The urge to coax sounds from the back of her throat: *eh, mauh, ah, ah, mauh, mauh.*

Alnes is simultaneously outside, observing this dissociated experience – as if from her mother's point of view – and inside, feeling her skull clouding: both the dispassionate observer and the participant. I find this approach both moving and revealing: I know the feeling of desperation as a mother of a child who is chronically ill, but it also helps me to have an insight into how it might feel from inside the illness experience. My daughter has been suffering with post-viral fatigue for a number of years, and I have to remind myself to sit with her illness, to observe as well as listen, to encourage her to speak and describe how it feels, rather than dismissing her, often for my own reasons – because I fear this illness; because I can't bear to see my daughter so helpless, a victim to whether or not her body is able to perform. Because I want her to be well again, and because my lack of control brings up my own deep fear of failing. Without meaning to, I find myself overwriting her illness experience, my own kind of gaslighting. (And I tuck it in here, because it is private, enveloped by the grander texts that surround it, and her story is also not my story to tell.)

Alnes goes on to write – in first person this time – that these episodes had in fact been happening since she was 18, 'after living a remarkably healthy life' when she fainted in her dorm, waking to see the world around her like 'a surrealist painter's vision: dressers spinning toward the white tiled ceiling, bed wobbling in my sight' and how this day marked the division between who she was and who she was to become. 'When I entered the doctor's office, I became a body. A set of symptoms. A story someone else told.' Like Atkin, Alnes draws our attention to how her doctor calls into question the reliability of her claims, 'She *apparently* sat down', 'she *denies* problems with self-esteem'. His medical knowledge gives him the authority to have the last word.

The braided form of this essay adds another layer of objectification. Alnes winds together narratives to create a different, more complex whole. In another, complementary narrative a historic story emerges, but one that has also been forgotten or misrepresented. It is on a school trip to Peru that Alnes first comes across the legend of the 'ice maiden' or 'Juanita', who had been given up to the Incas as a sacrifice and mummified: 'a story born of science and artifact'. Alnes identifies with the folkloric girl's lost past because she too has had to stitch together her own identity and her own lost past via artefacts, an archaeology of her own: a marathon bib, a travel wheelchair, medical reports.

In 'What Remains', Alnes sets about finding her own story and her own way of writing it, and the act of writing becomes reclamation ('From this collection in my living room, the ghost of a girl takes shape') and the best way to do this is to let the body speak for itself, falling in fragments on to the page:

'brain clenched fist too tight and pulsing'.

Being a reader of writing like this is a little like eavesdropping, opening a door on an inner life, which is truthful, private and intimate. It has a similar spontaneous quality to *vérité* filmmaking, otherwise known as *cinéma vérité*, 'truthful cinema' – which aspires to capture an experiential truth of a situation by following the people who live it. These films are poetic rather than propaganda, immediate rather than explanatory, the narrative sublimated in action. A British filmmaker who does this well is Andrea Arnold, whose close, intimate shots touch the nerve of experience.

In her extraordinary memoir, *Bandit*, Molly Brodak similarly explores a dissociated experience, as if she's stepping into an underworld, a place of sensory and bodily feeling, after a seven-hour surgery to remove a tumour that had grown behind her eyes. But surprisingly, she is grateful for her new sense of headlessness: 'Now on the bed I was awake but I was somewhere new in my body. My head was gone. That *I* that lived here had moved down and "*I*" was in my chest and stomach.' In this new-found state she feels lucky to let go of the cerebral noise of self-doubt that had plagued her all her life. She has become 'rich from decapitation. More advantaged than those still attached to that awful organ.' Instead, she is left in 'just quietness. Sunk into a ground, a bed, as I had sometimes dreamed, in real liminality now ...'. I find this passage one of the most honest and moving in Brodak's memoir, particularly in light of her suicide four years after *Bandit* was published.

Cristín Leach in her memoir *Negative Space* finds somatic language for the everyday struggles of being a woman and a mother, while grieving the end of her marriage. 'The language of small children rearing is a language of body and sound,' she writes. 'I sang my comfort and my anguish to my kids. They cried their needs to me.' She also writes of the violation she feels when having a cervical smear, and the absence of words for this violation, instead processing it by drawing a comic strip, a simple line drawing. 'A chimney brush pushed through the mouth of a bottle'. This violent act is at the hands of the doctors, her body not her own, whereas when giving birth her body comes into its power, finding its own language and expression: the sounds one makes in childbirth can help open the cervix to help the baby along; how interconnected are the throat with the vagina and cervix; what a genius design. 'Let go of all head-based decisions and become only body and sound,' she writes. The body in birth speaks in impulses. It is abstract, driven by instinct and emotion. It teaches us so much. To understand it is to enter into bodily sensations; to feel the swimming nausea of pain, the clench of contraction, the ache and the burn.

A Ghost in the Throat, by Doireann Ní Ghríofa, a hybrid of memoir, autofiction, criticism and history, literally exploits the idea of the throat as the source of emotion and femaleness. Her narrator is obsessed with the *keening* of a (real) eighteenth-century poet lost to history, Eibhlín Dubh Ní Chonaill, and the book follows her quest to bring the poet back into cultural consciousness, both her texts, but also her being in embodied form. Every page you turn concerns the body: the embodiment and disembodiment of early motherhood and birth; her carnal desire for her husband; breast pumping for milk banks; the stench of dead bodies in a dissection room. Despite Eibhlín Dubh Ní Chonaill having been a ghostly presence in Ní Ghríofa's life since she came across her lament 'Caoineadh Airt Uí Laoghaire' in her school days, and despite her having been known only as an appendage to the men in her life – someone's sister, someone's wife – to Ní Ghríofa

she was 'as real as any other unseen presence – as real as
the disembodied voices on the radio, as real as the human
chorus on the internet, as real as the roots stretching
unseen under weeds', and she affectionately refers to her
as 'Nelly'. Ní Ghríofa sets to task to bring the poet back
into being, but also back into history, through letters,
journal entries and court proceedings, as a woman and
a person in her own right. But it's the memoir aspect of
this story, and the way Ní Ghríofa combines the poet's
stories with her own, that makes it stand out from a
simple historical reimagining.

A key influence throughout the book is the writer and
feminist critic Hélène Cixous, and especially her essay
'The Laugh of the Medusa', from which Ní Ghríofa quotes:
'Woman must put herself into the text – as into the world
and into history – by her own movement.' In order to do
this, women must find their own specific language, and
move away from the conventional patriarchal systems,
their self-identity evolving through the body. Part of this
process, according to Cixous, happens through writing
from within the female body, writing with breast milk
as metaphorical 'white ink'. Memoir, with its leaning
towards subjectivity and deeply felt expression, is not
simply about finding voice, and being heard, it can be a
political move too. As the essayist Patricia Hampl writes:
'Memoir must be written because each of us must have
a created version of the past. To transform experience
into meaning and value. If we refuse to do this, someone
else will do it for us. What is remembered is what becomes
reality.'

But what if your attempts to follow the impulse of
illness and lean into its own unique voice leaves you

floundering, unsure of what form you are writing and for whom? There is an increased interest in what might be classed as 'hybrid' writing, which blends and blurs definitions like fiction, non-fiction, poetry, prose, screenwriting. It is a mongrel form, boundless, with fuzzy borders, existing between spaces, on the edge of things, beyond the city limits (and I'm not talking suburban). Machado's *In the Dream House*, for instance, combines memoir with speculative fiction, borrowing and manipulating tropes from the literary genres of horror, fantasy and science fiction. Memoirs made up of poetry would also fit into this category, like Julia Bell's *Hymnal*, a memoir in verse, which Julia describes as a series of snapshots of rural Welsh life, almost like a photo album, which was inspired by her love for the 'uniquely poetic' Welsh language of her childhood. Another book that springs to mind is Mary J. Oliver's *Jim Neat*, which is a collage of archival documents, like letters, lists, prison records, diaries, postcards, photographs, various other people's points of view of an elusive father; devoid of a narrative persona, it is not a memoir as we know it, but it is also not really a biography, following the chronology of a life with narrative comment and explanation. Hybrid forms attempt to find their own deeply personal form and language for experience.

In a *Guardian* review, Olivia Laing describes Jenn Ashworth's *Notes Made While Falling* as an anti-memoir, or a personal account that refuses the personal. Ashworth had initially intended to write a novel about the traumatic labour of her second child, but she couldn't get beyond writing in note form. The more she worked on it, the more it resisted any kind of story shape, and she almost abandoned it entirely. What we are left with is a hybrid work, what she calls a 'mishmash of failed ways of telling'. But it has the magpie quality of the transliminal, picking up and protecting the shining gems of revelation, through personal recollection, speculative fiction, appropriation of fiction by others as a way of exploring her experience through other perspectives, and cultural and academic criticism. Ashworth avoids dwelling on the events themselves – in fact, as she tells me, she goes 'through all kinds of contortions to avoid it'. Instead we as readers are viscerally thrown about in a fitful re-enacting of experience, nervy and unsettled. 'I wanted to show how it was possible to be very sick, very distressed and still be able to think, to consider, to reflect – at the same time. Reminding myself of that was comforting: I'd lost my mind and not lost my mind, all at once.'

Because past trauma can smack back into consciousness with such immediacy, persistent presence and lucidity – as if it were happening in the now – it disrupts and subverts chronology. After all, where does past trauma end? In some cases, the act of writing reopens old wounds, might even bring buried memories back into consciousness. There is sometimes a good reason for forgetting, particularly after child sexual abuse. As Leigh Gilmore writes, 'it is an adaptive response to an abusive situation; children need to trust the adults who care for them'. Writing memoir, remembering a buried past, can bring pain and discomfort, and for some it can be devastating. But for many it is necessary.

The Missing List by Clare Best is the clearest example I have read of a memoir that finds its own unique and hybrid way to express the unspeakable, not just as a personal quest – although like all the best creative projects it starts off like that – but also to stand in for other survivors of incestuous sexual abuse, who have been silenced or have forgotten for their own self-preservation. The process of rediscovering her lost memories from a traumatic childhood was set in motion only in the mid-1990s when she was serving as a juror in a case of child sexual abuse. She began 'writing scraps of old memories … fragments. I had no idea what to do with them or even what they were,' she tells me. But, in the same way that Alnes rediscovered her lost memory through artefacts, Best proceeds in her own personal archaeology. What evolves is a collage – diary entries of the months leading to her father's death in the present-day story; a transcript of her father talking about his life; memories often told thematically, or through motif (for instance writing about her mother by writing about various kitchens) and descriptions of scenes depicted through cine film footage. Later in the narrative, she turns to her school reports, measuring them against a scrapbook her mother kept. This piecing together represents what Best describes as 'my fragmented emotional life'. Any other rendering of the story would have felt artificial and disloyal to a lifetime of living with part memories, buried secrets, flashes.

> Secrets. Hard heavy things that have long been packed carefully in layers of silence. The secrets have become more and more closed, the wrapping more minutely folded and sealed. Promises and silences, known and kept … This silence enclosing the secrets used to be my resting place. Blank and calm and numb and knowing no words. Simply being.

Best tells me that her memories were different in nature from other people's memories, and it took a long time before she was able to understand why. 'There were certain

images and feelings that kept intruding into my consciousness, like something rising out of deep water. Often these
images of feelings didn't have any words attached, so
"writing" them was odd and difficult. I realised much
later that many of these phenomena were sensory and
somatic memories from early childhood. They caused me
to feel agitated and sometimes unwell.' By following her
feeling self, Best creates what becomes an essential case
study of a complex and nuanced transgressive family
relationship. There is no attempt to make it anything
other than what it is – the reality is that the story is
faulted, full of holes, disruption, questioning, uncertainty.
There is no resolution from living with this level of trauma.
It just is.

But it is important to have distance if you are writing
through illness or trauma. Atkin could write *Some of Us
Just Fall* only after she had received a proper diagnosis,
and Best began to interrogate her buried memories only in
middle age, when her father was dying. It takes distance to
reflect and to find language. G. Thomas Couser in his book
Recovering Bodies: Illness, Disability and Life Writing,
writes that the relationship 'between bodily dysfunction
and personal narrative is complex'. Experiencing illness
and coming closer to death can have paradoxical effects.
On the one hand it might make one's consciousness
more vivid, and on the other it might be obstructive. As
Couser points out, only a small fraction of ill and disabled
people will ever write their stories, because so many will
be too ill or too traumatised to do so. 'Illness and disability might turn people so far inward that they become
virtual black holes, absorbing energy rather than emitting
illumination.'

I needed distance to write *Sins of My Father*, because I needed to find my voice, and my authority to tell a story about having my voice subsumed by the needs of a narcissistic father. I also had to find the confidence to speak for a father, a patriarch, a natural authority as my parent. But in the last years of his life, my father 'turned inwards' (to use Couser's phrase) and became a 'virtual black hole' of suffering. His body stopped working after years of alcohol and prescription-drug dependence, and liver damage affected his brain. The snake of addiction had taken him, and he had lost self-awareness. He was reduced to his impulses and his needs, needs that were killing him. He was living the 'chaos story', as Frank describes it. 'The voice of the teller has been lost as a result of the chaos, and this loss then perpetuates that chaos ...'. According to Frank, 'those who are truly living the chaos cannot tell in words.' The chaos story needs to be told retrospectively, or by someone else. When my father died of alcoholism, he became incapable of telling his own story. But his story was important to me and, it turned out, to other children of narcissist parents, who had been seduced by the 1970s promise of liberalism; those who had hit the hippy trail, had joined cults, had buried their eventual displacement in hedonism (there are many of them). By the end of his illness, my father was too ill to tell, or even recognise, his story. What if my telling his story helped make sense of something he was not able to make sense of himself?

My narrative then becomes what Frank calls a 'quest narrative'. 'The quest narrative speaks from the ill person's perspective and holds chaos at bay.' My dad of course would never have told his story the way I wrote it, because it was told from a daughter's point of view; worse still, a daughter who had felt betrayed by him. But within my quest to write the story was a need to make sense of events that had felt inconceivable. How could a man who had had everything – wealth, success, emotional awareness, a beautiful house in a desirable seaside town in California, a lovely wife – have squandered it all so catastrophically?

I remember meeting with my PhD supervisor and friend Julia Bell after she had read my book and she had tears in her eyes when she said to me, 'you gave your father dignity in writing about him'. I was deeply touched; but maybe, by giving words to the unspeakable, I had also given form to something that might otherwise have been lost to history. My father had died alone on the floor of a B&B, and I was not prepared for that to be the final curtain.

Frank's hypothesis rings true, that the 'wounded storyteller' becomes empowered through their storytelling, when 'story transforms fate into experience', and the self begins to shift and change through what is being understood. My father's fate was suffering; my telling his story with care and compassion gave meaning to what had become meaningless and catastrophic. Through this process I grew and changed, and in many ways began to heal those wounds I had held on to for so long, because this story for the first time was my story. I stepped up, and by doing so I invited other people to step up, too; because they related to my story, they could begin to think about their own, which they too might have previously found impossible. When this transformation is shared, whether through speaking or through writing, 'the disease that sets the body apart from others becomes, in the story, the common bond of suffering that joins bodies in their shared vulner-ability'. This, in turn, strengthens the bonds of community. I had also been the ill person – not ill with alcoholism, but ill with the trauma of being the child of an addict. When you speak out, you are no longer the victim, no longer voiceless; instead, you harness the power that comes from shared experience and recognise that in being wounded, and sharing that experience, you have the capacity to become a healer too.

It can be difficult to access challenging emotion. What if you are driven to write about a situation that has affected you, but every time you commit words to the page it falls apart? Maybe the emotion is difficult to access on demand, or maybe it can't be accessed at all, because it is too shameful or too painful – the body and mind do an excellent job of blocking feeling out.

Try this:

1. A good place to start is to write a short paragraph about something you were afraid to tell your mother or father when you were growing up. This will most likely be a dark secret, which shame and embarrassment might have buried deep within you. Once it is out on the page, it might not look so bad.
2. Now I want you to reflect on why you find this secret so painful to own up to. What is it about you or your family, or the relationship you have with this part of yourself that is difficult to sit with? Write into it. Try to capture the feeling and write from within it. What does shame look like? What does it feel like? Can you embody it, or find symbol to stand in for it?

3. Now have a think about how writing about this subject might be helpful to your readers. What is more important, burying the truth of this secret, or starting a discussion so that others might find the courage to transcend their own pain?

Or try the hermit crab essay.

If you still find it difficult to write about, then why not consider experimenting with a hybrid essay? The hermit crab is an essay structure which is designed to bury the difficult stuff in its shell. In fact, the hermit crab crawls into a shell and grows to fill it, taking the contours as its own. I am not going to ask you to be a crab, but to find an existing form – it could be a recipe or a shopping list, or the list of side effects in your medication. What type of form relates to the secret you want to write about but are afraid to expose?

One of my favourite examples of the hermit crab essay is 'The Heart as a Torn Muscle' by Randon Billings Noble, which playfully explores the stigma of falling in love with someone when you are in a relationship with someone else. In an interview for the Brevity Blog, Billings Noble talks of how she went on a writing residency and damaged her back. 'I had been sketching an essay about temptation and heartbreak and was thinking of structuring it as a timeline,' she says. 'How long does it take to get over a crush, especially a forbidden one? ... Then I started to think about my back and how long it took to heal. Could a heart heal in the same time span? After doing some seemingly unrelated, very practical and non-literary research about ice packs and anti-inflammatories, I realized that the heart, too, is a muscle. And much of what I was reading about an actual torn muscle started to feel relevant to treating a metaphorically torn heart. I took the structure from various medical advice sites and wrote from there.'

The structure of this essay is not only funny, but also acts as a protective shape for the sensitive material explored. You can tweak and subvert the material in order to fit the form. Then the very act of constraining the material should liberate it – it might help you take some risks! I did this with my undergraduate students recently and they loved the idea of transplanting their experience into something surprising and playful.

Back bedroom - makeshift MOF-
Dad sat at one end & mum at other
& we moved to at CW at 6pm & they
worked. & Mum read what she'd write
that day o dad at night.

Mum had a dream in middle g which
& thinkg of at all the time. Coleridge
Came to Mum in the dream & Said g
Corrie. May was eclipsed by Shelley
where you find g caste near my Whee

meani _____ eclipse. of use
the mun _____ when in light g
its own _____ o in he said he
was the _____ fire & she watte
reply _____ eclipse mysterou
mum

5

The holder of the threads: who is speaking and where are they standing?

During the years before my marriage separation, I went weekly to a Jungian analyst. I hadn't wanted to start therapy. I was of the camp that believed it was impossibly expensive, an indulgence – where would I find the money? – or a sign that there was something wrong with me, something I had failed to deal with. But I know now looking back, I was also afraid of what therapy would unearth. I was afraid of taking action. If I stayed absolutely still, everything would remain the same and no one would be hurt.

But over time I learned to reflect and stand apart from the landscape of my story. I was not simply in the centre of a storm, a participant in the drama, victim to destructive forces; circumstance came from choice – way had led to way had led to way. I began to engage with my power and my agency: if I had made choices that had brought me here, I could make choices to make it better. I could see how my unhappiness had a trajectory, and the landscape was a kind of weaving, a working together of various coloured threads. One thread was the voice that kept telling me to leave, which only got louder when I ignored it; I realised it was telling me something important. What if it was a voice of inner wisdom, the subconscious rising up to guide me? Instructive, rather than destructive. What if it was the golden thread, the part that was brighter and more valuable than the others? Even in the worst of the storm, it guided me with its iridescence over the threshold into my new life, and remained a constant through the challenges of building that life for me and my children. That voice, that thread, became essential for my personal growth, but also for my memoir writing. Good memoirs have clarity of voice, and hard-won insight and wisdom. Honesty is the guiding principle, and the reader will pick up on a writer who is lacking conviction or is deceiving themselves.

As we saw in the chapter, 'From the static into the moving world', memoir is often made up of both participatory scenes in action, and the self-aware, probing voice of wisdom. I knew that I had to get in touch with my observer, my noticing self, so she could become the organising principle in a life that had spun out of control, and she was also essential for my writing. I had been driven to leave my marriage for my own happiness. A selfish act. In ancient Indian Vedic drama, the director is known as the holder of the threads. By leaving on my terms, I had become the director of my life, but also of my story. I needed to take responsibility, and be ready to weave those threads together.

There is nowhere to hide when writing memoir, and therefore honesty and voice are everything. When I say voice, I mean the narrator's personality, and how they deliver their experience to the reader, but I also mean the clarity of intention, and the right tone, straddling humility and authority, self-awareness and compassion for oneself as well as those you are writing about. It is no easy task. Just as it isn't easy to know yourself, and good memoir demands that a narrator knows herself well enough to stand by her narrative as her own version of events. To find the greater, universal meaning in those events she must engage with her own particular wisdom, and then assert that wisdom with confidence.

Finding your voice is finding yourself within the narrative, finding your authority as the person telling this tale, and therefore finding your position from which to tell it, the best point of entry, the best frame, the best bandwidth with the most clarity. This chapter is primarily about how we find that authority and give ourselves permission to step into our narrative and call it our own. This can be slow and difficult, particularly for voices that have been subsumed or overwritten, as we saw in the previous chapter. Because for some writers it takes time to truly get to know their writerly self, and for some to even recognise it. But be patient. This process, I have found, is essential to the development of a memoir, and can even be woven into its telling.

So many writers I teach and mentor clasp their head in their hands and ask: *why am I doing this? Who cares about my story – why does anyone care?* The first step, perhaps, is to realise that no one will care, unless you care. So I always ask my students to first try to engage with why the story matters to them. Why is it important to *me?* Then the journey begins. Mostly, you won't know at the start of a book project. It can take many drafts, and many years to work it out. Because clarity of voice is tied in with clarity of vision, and a proper understanding and mastering of what a particular story is about, voice – I find – will follow. Joan Didion wrote in *Why I Write* that writing is an aggressive and hostile act. The act of writing 'I' on the page, stating your view, 'imposing oneself upon other people, of saying listen to me, see it my way, change your mind' – is an invasion of one's opinion into someone else's world – 'an imposition of the writer's sensibility on the reader's most private space'. This takes a huge amount of confidence.

This is why I chose to place this chapter towards the end of the book. Voice, and the ability to stand by one's narrative, are closely aligned with emotion and a readiness, or preparedness, in you as the narrator to harness your power. To find your voice, you must go to the place in yourself that you need to go to, to tell the story that needs to be told. There are so many reasons why you might not want to do this. Firstly, you might instinctively turn away from the truth, particularly if it is difficult and confronting, or if it involves your loved ones having to go back into the past alongside you, whether they want to or not. Or it might be that somehow you missed the truth, or you're not yet able to see clearly enough to recognise it.

In an early draft of my memoir, I was convinced the story started in the right place. In the narrative, my mother phones me to tell me that my father has died, and my toddler daughter crawls across the floor towards me. This felt like the perfect paradox, finally the end of my father's protracted suffering just as I have everything lined up to support the burgeoning life of my own family. I felt both sadness and relief. But when I chose that point of entry, I hadn't yet realised what a grip my father still had on me, one that reached into my marriage and my years of early motherhood that caused me to divorce, that followed me even to my new life – so tentatively built, with my new partner in Bristol. I was still living the story, and there were still a few years to live before I would have a clearer grasp of my father's effect on me, and therefore of the story and my place in it.

Robin, who is a screenwriter, believed that there was a more dramatic place to start, which was when my dad got embroiled in a scam. From a dramatic point of view he was right, as the book had evolved into a dual biography by this time – my father's story eclipsing mine. Robin felt the scam was the point of no return, when my father began his descent to rock bottom. And though in the existing narrative I had placed it chronologically, about two-thirds of the way through, he suggested I bring it to the forefront as an inciting incident. I rewrote the scam episode and it made for a dramatic start. But what about me? The storyteller telling this tale. What was the point of it? I was the narrator, the director, the holder of the threads. I had to ask myself: where am I standing? Why am I returning to these events that happened ten or so years ago? What do I *feel* about it all?

It was not until the final draft of writing *Sins of My Father* that I began to 'lean into the text' as the author Marina Benjamin calls it, where you bring to the page your opinion, your view, your authority as the person writing the story. I have come to realise I am not alone in my struggle to give myself permission to do this: when teaching memoir, time and again, I hear women writers particularly saying that growing up they were not encouraged to have an opinion, or to think their opinion mattered. What gives them the right to write this story? Let alone step up into the narrative and claim the story as their own? This results in writing that lacks the personal or personality edge – the identifiable voice that will make your reader feel as if they are sitting and listening to a friend. A memoir without a clearly defined voice also lacks the kind of assertiveness that personal narrative needs for its authority to teach the reader something. *I know this. This is what I believe.*

If I wrote this as a novel, I might have got away with just writing the events themselves, letting the story unfold. But as memoir, which often has a 'telling' component, as well as 'showing', I knew I needed to engage more with my quest. After many years, and reworking, my starting position in the narrative came to me as a devastating gift. A simple visit from my brother in my new home, well after I had written the first draft. He said he did not want to read my memoir, and I was upset. I was mostly taken aback because I realised I had written it to try to share my understanding of our father and the possible reasons he had made certain choices in his life; but of course that was only my perspective – I hadn't considered my brother had not asked for this. His refusal helped me identify my emotional position, and it also brought into stark light the difference between us, how we dealt with the loss of our father in our own personal ways. It was the first time I saw the story from my brother's point of view, and in understanding this I could better understand my own. It also made me connect with why I felt such a driving need to write the book.

When my brother told me he did not want to read my book, I was propelled into reflecting on why it was so important for me to write it. This became my quest, along with my attempt to answer the question of whether it was better to confront the pain of the past, or to bury it. This question set the story in motion, and my attempts to answer it brought the past and present together. I had my reason to write the book, and this clarity fed into a confidence in my voice. I leaned into the text because it suddenly mattered.

Sitting on the sidelines of a narrative also clouds story. In *The Situation and the Story*, Vivian Gornick argues that one of the main purposes of memoir is to better understand the self, by interrogating the subject in hand, whether that's addiction, systemic racism or intergenerational trauma. 'The writing we call personal narrative is written by people who, in essence, are imagining only themselves: in relation to the subject in hand.' And part of better understanding the self is to approach yourself with scrutiny, to take responsibility for your actions, and mistakes. It takes great confidence to see yourself in the round like this, and it takes discipline. Joan Didion speaks of this in her essay 'On Self Respect': 'people with self-respect exhibit a certain toughness, a kind of moral nerve, they display what was once called character ... [and] character – the willingness to accept responsibility for one's life – is the source from which self-respect springs'.

A lot of the difficultly that I had in leaning into the narrative in the early drafts of my memoir was because I'd had my feelings undermined by a narcissistic father who had not treated me with respect. I simply wasn't used to speaking up and trusting my instinct. When you have had your instinct undermined by those closest to you – when you lack what psychoanalyst Sándor Ferenczi calls an 'empathetic witness' to help you differentiate right from wrong – you don't grow up to trust yourself, and therefore don't assert yourself, and your opinions continue to be subsumed by others. It took me many years to take responsibility for myself, and to see that my opinion mattered. But through my writing and reading memoir, and the research I was doing on my PhD, I realised that I was not an isolated being and that many other people had been through similar (and a lot worse!), and I began to grow in confidence. I felt held by other people's stories and the collective experience.

As a teenager, I spent my summers visiting my father, who ran a community and a publishing business in a beautiful Tuscan villa. One summer, one of his friends groomed me and tried to have sex with me (I was 13 and a virgin). I always had a hunch that this cannot have been an isolated event, as it seemed so strange to me, even then, that this man would think it his right to ask this of me, and also that my father appeared to condone it. It felt so removed from the normal happenings of my everyday life at home in London with my mother. But the experience of visiting my dad was often disorientating. It was a different world, with high emotions and a lack of boundaries or rules. It was both troubling and intoxicating. Throughout my father's involvement with the cult of Rajneeshism, I had visited him in various communes – Oak Village in London, then Medina in Suffolk and later his house in Italy and surrounding communities in Tuscany. I hung about the kids who grew up in these communes, and found them intimidating and beguiling; they were sexually mature and provocative. After this event at my father's house, I was beginning to question why.

When Tim Guest's memoir, *My Life in Orange*, was published, the reality of young kids having sex way too young within the communes was finally brought to light. I see now that it was obvious that if you grew up in a 'sex cult' you would copy what your parents were doing, certainly with each other. The fact that this extended to men having sex with young girls felt too transgressive to be spoken freely, but I began to look for signs in Osho's discourse of sexual initiation between adult and child. When I published a personal essay with Aeon about my experience that summer, many women tracked me down and thanked me for speaking out. It was validating for them, but in turn validating for me. It was this that gave me the confidence to go further in my memoir. I was beginning to tap into a collective experience, and the writing had a purpose beyond being curative for myself.

When a stream of testimonies written by those who had grown up in the Rajneesh communes landed on Facebook pages just before my book was published, my deepest fears were met, but also my hunch was right. The grooming of children and condoning of sexual initiation between an adult and a child was widespread; it was part of the culture, and even more extreme than I had imagined. Reading these testimonies was re-triggering, but also empowering. I had to go through the pain of reliving my own sense of powerlessness and confusion as a child in order to come out the other side. As time progressed and the adults started to acknowledge their part in this crime, apologising to those who had been abandoned and abused, and beginning to question their own motivations, my own pain at my father's betrayal started to fade, and a new feeling took its place. It was one of anger. For the first time, I knew in my bones that what had happened to me as a child was wrong, that it was part of a culture of abuse, and that it only touched the surface of what other children had had to endure. I could now take a moral high ground, and this clarity showed itself in my writing. I could make use of the anger, coupled with a growing and curious compassion. I was beginning to better understand my father, even after his death.

My memoir was picked up quickly by Jenny Lord, the publishing director at Weidenfeld & Nicolson, part of Orion. After reading the full manuscript for the first time, she had little editorial comment except for one key thing, which would ultimately shift the focus of the book. At the time the book was called *Starman*, a title I really loved, and which I felt encapsulated my father's personality which was otherworldly in lots of ways, ungrounded, disconnected, drifting off in his ulterior reality, whether through the science-fiction books he had written, his cult antics or his eventual addiction to prescription drugs and alcohol. But my editor had read it differently. To her, the image of Starman was iconic, created by the equally iconic David Bowie, and it rang too much of how I still, despite everything, put my father on a pedestal. 'Your father is not a Starman,' she said. She was afraid that my reader would feel that I was too willing and ready to forgive him his transgressions, and that this image of the Starman somehow excused him.

Although this feedback was difficult to hear, it nudged me and forced open a space in my psyche, and I found myself dreaming of my father one night when I was at the crucial stage of final edits. In my dream the two words 'bad dad' drifted into my consciousness. I realised more deeply that I knew my father was bad, but I had never really been able to admit it to myself because it felt too scary – and if my father was bad, what did that make me? In the end, I incorporated this journey of coming to better know myself through the redrafting of my memoir into my final chapter. To this day, I acknowledge that this deeper reading of my memoir could have been done only by someone other than me, and someone professional (and emotionally astute) because it was a comment that dug into the very foundation of my relationship with my father, too deeply set in history and familial dysfunction for me to clearly see.

It is empowering to be in control of your story, giving yourself the task to try to discover and understand. When I finally found that voice it was like magic. The voice was my guide, and she led me through the story with intention and confidence so that the reader knew exactly what I wanted them to take from the text – it was my text, my story, my book.

But the process of finding one's writerly voice is different for all writers. For the author Jade Angeles Fitton, when writing her memoir, *Hermit*, the voice was always there. She told me how the first chapters in the published book were the first chapters she ever wrote for it – but it was a matter of finding the confidence to use it. At first, she hid behind the research, before her editor urged her to step more into the text, so that her reader could fully identify with why she found her time living in solitude so transformative. This involved her writing about an abusive relationship that had preceded this period, which made Jade feel very uncomfortable. In order to do this, she had to 'remove the vulnerable part of myself while writing it – disconnect from it, which I think anyone who has gone through a trauma develops a (slightly unhealthy) knack for'.

Fitton tells me she gets up early to write before the world wakes up, and she writes from an instinctive part of herself – 'it feels like an old part of me; it is more ego-less … and has no qualms about revealing embarrassing or shameful things about myself'. In those early hours, she is able to tap into a part of herself she doesn't show in her everyday life – which is great for the writing and for the story, but can be uncomfortable when the book is published and this more private part of the self is put out into the world. She gets around this with a positive attitude, and one of healthy detachment. This story might be relevant now, she says, but in another few years there will be another story. Fitton is not the story – in its evolution, the story becomes something else. She has a lovely way of articulating this: 'Writing is like the distillation of experience. If it were a stone, it would be quartz – the hardest most sparkling bits that are left after everything else is worn away.'

The author and memoirist Marina Benjamin agrees that voice tends to become truer the longer you have worked on a project. She says that voice is so tricky because it needs to be both authentic and performative – it must be tapping into an author's truth while simultaneously telling a story. But, we must avoid getting self-conscious in the process because self-consciousness, according to Benjamin, is the enemy of authenticity. One way that she helps herself in the early stages of writing is to 'write behind my own back'. She opens what she calls 'low temperature files' where she will free-write, keeping the writing private. The privacy is crucial here – much like writing in a journal – as privacy often leads to freedom of expression. But when Benjamin uses the word 'truthful' she doesn't mean 'factually true' or even faithful to memory. 'I mean intimate, transparent, open. And by transparent, incidentally, I mean self-aware, absent of self-regard.'

For Benjamin it is not so important at an early stage to get it right, but more to make it real, in the way that automatic writing often bypasses the self-critical and obstructive voices that can get in the way of a heartfelt connection with your subject. Raw experience is transformed into language, and language liberates. By speaking, we begin to understand better. A story starts to unfold. This transmuting process cannot happen without a willingness in its author to question their experience and begin to understand it differently. As Vivian Gornick says: 'The memoirist ... must engage with the world, because engagement makes experience, experience makes wisdom, and finally it's the wisdom – or rather the movement towards it – that counts.'

When discovering story, it helps, I find, to be aware of yourself sitting at your desk and writing from the 'now', engaging with your reflective voice, and the wisdom of what you have come to know and to understand, and your motivation for wanting to write this story. This, as we saw in the chapter 'From the static into the moving world', allows for more freedom and flexibility: from that anchored point you can jump backwards and forwards, allowing the text to echo the meandering nature of memory, with transliminal leaps of the imagination between linked associations, research and showing these workings of the mind on the page. 'A memoir is a work of sustained narrative prose controlled by an idea of the self under obligation to lift from the raw material of life a tale that will shape experience, transform event, deliver wisdom,' Gornick writes in *The Situation and the Story*. The writer is obliged to go beyond the simple telling of event or anecdote, to the meaning buried beneath. 'What happened to the writer is not what matters,' writes Gornick. 'What matters is the large sense that the writer is able to *make* of what happened.' Movement and drama in a memoir evolve not from cause and effect, but from the author's slow dawning of realisation and clarity.

None of this is to say that all memoirs should be reflective – there are plenty of good ones that are written in the present tense from the child's point of view, told chronologically, the narrator's voice maturing as the story progresses. Of contemporary memoirs, Tiffany Murray's *My Family and Other Rock Stars* and Ali Millar's *The Last Days* come to mind. But despite there being no reflective voice, the author's wisdom and hindsight pulses in the selected detail. First-person present tense can feel quite limiting, having to follow events as they happened, and Murray gets around this by including her mother's recipes, to bring variety to the text, but also to bring in her mother's voice from the past. Additionally, Murray interviews her mother, who looks back to her own past. This enables the main narrative to remain mostly in the early 1970s to the early 1980s, when her mother was chef to two famous rock recording studios. Ali Millar has an interesting perspective on the reflective voice, saying she purposefully avoided it because it can be tyrannical. She says: 'I wanted the reader to reflect on it [her book] rather than being told what to reflect on.' Reading Millar's memoir is an immersive experience because we are invited into the world of a child who is isolated by circumstance, in the Jehovah's Witness cult, and we are with her, looking over her shoulder, as she grows up.

There is a lot of skill in writing a memoir in present tense. Often they have a filmic quality, and are those memoirs that are most closely aligned with fiction – bringing scenes vividly to life with good characterisation, dialogue and scene-setting. But I personally love the intimate, often exploratory and instructive nature of the reflective voice, and honour it as that which sets memoir apart. I often annotate memoirs that I love, and it is mostly the wise observations from the 'voice of wisdom', or reflective voice, that attract my attention. Reaching for the book nearest to me on my desk, I open *Splinters*, by Leslie Jamison. The first turned-over corner and underline reveals this: 'It was easier to crawl back into the bond that had always come most naturally to me, anyway – mother and daughter. My mom was the only person to whom I'd ever been able to say, boldly, plainly, without equivocation, *Please help me.*' This observation of Jamison's relationship with her mother is perceptive, sensitive, hard won. It is not something she would have known at the time of asking for help, but only when drawing back to the more detached perspective of adulthood with all that the mature Jamison has come to understand. Implicit in this statement is trust between a mother and daughter, but also Jamison's ability to see the emotional patterns of the relationship played out over time, with a writer's curiosity and eventual clarity.

This is one of the more conclusive statements in Jamison's memoir, and there are many others that are suggestive, and ask questions. The next paragraph is more exploratory, a nugget of beauty that reveals character through metaphor, all the while pointing to the theme of the memoir, which is motherhood and walking away from a conventional family before it has had a chance to establish itself:

> When I was a kid, I liked to write fairy tales with unhappy endings. The dragon roasted everyone. Or else the princess left her prince standing at the altar and flew away in a hot-air balloon over the sea. Maybe this was a happy ending, just a different kind. Not a wedding, but an untethering. Sandbags hurled over the edge of the basket. Flames blooming under silk.

It is less direct, yes, but it is no less wise, no less able to stand apart from the emotion explored and see it in image, and metaphor.

This level of wisdom and self-awareness is essential to writing memoir and comes from doing the difficult work, trying to understand and articulate emotion (Jamison does refer to having a therapist). As author and teacher, Julia Bell said to me when I first embarked on writing personal narrative, 'You need to do the work on yourself before taking it to the page; your reader does not want to have to do the difficult work for you.' No one wants to read a narrator who isn't seeing what feels obvious to a reader – and this comes back to clarity of intent and self-knowledge. As Mary Karr says in *The Art of Memoir*, 'the writer who's lived a fairly unexamined life – someone who's had a hard time reconsidering a conflict from another point of view – may not excel at fashioning a voice because her defensiveness stands between her and what she has to say'.

But also, we change as we grow older. To use the relationship we have with our mothers as an example: this will change dramatically as we grow in our understanding of ourselves and of our mother, in her parental role but also as a human being with faults and flaws like anyone. As memoirists, we need to nurture our awareness of this change, so that we can distinguish between the view we might have had as a child, how that changed through adolescence, as a young adult, into middle age, and so on. This is all about perspective, where we position ourselves in the story and how that affects the story's telling. Truth and voice then become dynamic, a living presence that shifts and changes over time.

Deborah Levy, in the series of books she calls 'Living Autobiography', has a distinct voice, surprising in its quirkiness, but also satisfying in its wisdom and self-knowledge. In *The Cost of Living*, the second in this series, she, like Jamison, explores the rupture of a marriage, and the challenge of creating a new life with teenage children and limited resources, exploring her inner emotions through metaphor and small everyday objects. Her tone is cool, detached and funny. 'It was futile to try to fit an old life into a new life. The old fridge was too big for the kitchen, the sofa too big for the lounge, the beds the wrong shape to fit the bedrooms.'

As anyone who has heard Levy speak in person or in interviews will know, her voice in person is very like her voice on the page, her personality unapologetically bursting through. This clarity of expression gives her a lot of power as a writer of memoir, simply because it gives her authority and helps the reader trust her. But what also stands out in Levy's narrative is her particular view of the world around her, unique to her, that which becomes her trademark. If someone says, I read a Deborah Levy book, others who have also read her will know that that probably entails something quirky – 'to amuse myself (there was no one else around) I began to think about the genre of the female nightdress in relation to plumbing' – and refreshing leaps of thought. We also might expect to find the transliminal in her casual, easeful reference to her reading: 'My own unhappiness was starting to become a habit, in the way that Beckett described sorrow becoming "a thing you can keep adding to all your life ... like a stamp or an egg collection".' But, as in the Jamison book, there are also bolts of distinct and precise wisdom. 'Their father and I agreed that we would live separately but we would always live together in the lives of our children. There are only loving and unloving homes. It is the patriarchal story that has been broken. All the same, most children who grow up in that story will struggle, along with everyone else, to compose another one.'

I underline paragraph after paragraph, observations that make me stop and think and reassess what up to now has been my narrative, a narrative that is influenced by the patriarchal world in which we live. After I left my marriage, I personally really struggled with reconciling myself with my children being raised outside the traditional nuclear family of both biological parents still together, living side by side for ever, but after inhabiting Levy's world – a strong woman who stands firm beside her choice – I find myself wondering at the alternatives, and begin to accept that those alternatives might be okay.

Clare Best writes of how there were several narrative voices in *The Missing List* from the start, 'sort of competing for airtime'. At first she experienced it as 'failure' to find the right voice for the memoir, but then she gave into it and let all the voices in, and began to see how it added layers to the narrative. As we saw in a previous chapter, *The Missing List* is made up of a collage of different elements: written accounts of family cine film footage, journal entries from the time when her father was dying, scraps of her childhood memories, lists of different kinds and passages of verbatim material transcribed from recordings of her father talking about his own early life. 'Each of these elements has its "voice" and in concert they make up the overall voice of the narrative. My sense of my own authority grew as I covered the ground of my creative and therapeutic journeys – a slow, painful process. [In *The Missing List*] I have remade myself by writing about my life.'

As Benjamin pointed out, when we write a narrative of our life, we must be performative, taking on a particular role in the storytelling, while also true to our deepest darkest desires and fears, to give our work that authentic and believable edge. And we all perform in our everyday lives, too, depending on whether we are at home, or in the office or at the school gates. Are you slightly different when you are with your partner, your boss, your kids? And what if you're sad? You'll behave in a different way to whether you are tired, or hungry or excited. Our writing, too, is influenced by all these shifts in mood. But voice cannot be manufactured. It is better to write freely in that first draft, and unselfconsciously, as Benjamin stresses, and then start an intimate conversation with your writing, recognising those parts of the personality you want to amplify or which are right for a particular scene or line of enquiry. A deep engagement with the self must come first.

Call it the authentic voice, the engagement with your writerly self, or just a willingness to run to the edge of the cliff and to jump, damn the consequences, it is scary because what if people don't like you? What if you are yourself on the page and the reader finds that irritating? This will happen. Some readers won't get along with your voice, just as they might not be drawn to you at a party (most likely they are not your type of person either.) And that is okay. Jenn Ashworth had an interesting response to this problem. In discussion, she told me she would prefer, of course, for people to like or admire her work rather than dislike it, but that she can't really publish anything unless she is okay with the idea of people finding it deficient. 'Not justifying it to myself and saying they're jealous or they didn't get it or didn't read well enough or something – but just totally accepting that there will be loads of people who are totally indifferent and some that really really don't like it.' Ashworth goes on to say that this is about her writing, but it's also about the way she inhabits the world: 'I can make friends with the fact that most people will be totally indifferent to my existence, some will like me, and some really won't. There's nothing about that situation that's dangerous or needs fixing, even though I might not exactly enjoy it sometimes.'

It might also help to tell yourself that just as many readers, if not more, will admire your courage, your transparency, your willingness to confront difficult emotions, so that they too might begin to confront their own. I have come to understand this courage as generosity. The willingness to share aspects of your life to help others do the same. And in practising this and realising how much readers appreciate it, you in turn will build in confidence and self-esteem.

Clover Stroud spoke to me about how often readers thank her for her openness as a writer, that her honesty allows them to identify and feel emotions that they might not previously had been able to articulate, whether it be grief or homesickness or a connection to family. 'When I wrote *The Wild Other*, which was in part about my mum's long-term brain damage following an accident, many people got in touch to say how reading it had enabled them to connect better with a family member. I find it consoling that one aspect of human suffering could, by sharing it, help ease another aspect of human confusion.' She goes on to say that when writing memoir, you're in a privileged position of being able to acutely analyse impactful events. 'And people often say: that's exactly what I was feeling. I just didn't really know it.'

It is also true that sometimes we discover our writerly voice only once our book is published and out there with readers. I only really discovered the quality of honesty and directness in my tone once readers and reviewers pointed it out. It felt crucial to me that my voice in *Sins of My Father* was crystal clear, particularly in contrast to the chaos that became my father's life; and honesty and straightness were my guiding principle as the daughter of a fantasist and liar. Non-fiction and specifically memoir appeal to me because of their transparent nature, because the reader values strength and clarity, because they will sniff out deception in a heartbeat. Because there is nowhere to hide.

Once I realised this and I owned this voice, once I 'leaned into the narrative', I was able to be much freer in my writing, to trust it and let go of the idea that I needed to have all the answers at the outset. Asking questions of experience, holding it up to the light, and using it as a springboard for new realisations not only helps bring the text alive, but also helps make sense of the past. I encourage my students to pause over key scenes, stop at important moments and ask themselves: what else? Have I said everything? What happened before this scene, what happened after, what was it like for those who exist off the page? Vivian Gornick takes this further by stating that 'exemplary memoir' is written by those who clearly ask, 'Who am I?' Not only this, but 'who exactly is this "I" upon whom turns the significance of this story-taken-directly-from-life? On that question the writer of memoir must deliver. Not with an answer but with depth of inquiry.' So begins your empathetic inquiry with yourself and your life as content, and therefore also with aspects of character or past experience you have never before explored.

Try this:

1. First of all, make a list that describes where you are from. What are your origins? What concrete details describe you and your family? For instance, I grew up in London in the 1970s and when I think of my

childhood, I think of pavements and London brick, a street that was my playground: hopscotch and running in and out of neighbours' houses. I can smell roses, either from my mother's small courtyard garden, or from the perfume she wore. The buildings are tall around me and sometimes they block out the light. I see the pavement more than I see the sky. (Be sure to slant your detail to mirror the emotions of this time in your life.)

2. Make another list (again using tangible objects) that describes where you are now – who you have become. Since I now live in Bristol, I don't quite get that sense of the street that I used to; things are more expansive here, and I notice the trees more, the brightness of the sun, and I search out the wilderness. I stand upright now, and the air tastes of green.

3. Write these lists freely, and let yourself move from childhood to school, to university, if you went, or your first job: try to capture those times with the same impressionistic detail. When I recall my time at university in Manchester, I see concrete, bricks and the orange of curry houses. The streets were often grey with rain, made more so in my imagination by my unhappiness there.

4. From this exercise you should have the beginning of yourself as a character who has shifted and changed throughout her life, but who notices certain things, and who is moved by others.

5. Now, focus in on one moment that has come to you through this exercise. I might write about my time playing out on the street and all the characters in our neighbourhood, picking out the detail of what we did

with each other. Or I might remember a certain event, like cooking chips to smuggle to the homeless person who lived in the derelict house at the end of our street. Focus in on that one moment that has caught your imagination and write it, but try to write it encompassing two elements: the voice of innocence, telling us all that happened at the time, and the voice of experience reflecting on that wisdom with hindsight.

Silvine

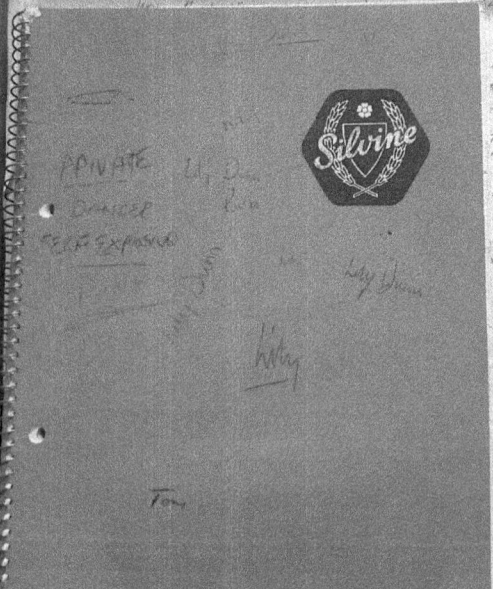

PRIVATE
DANGER
SELF EXPOSED

STUDENTS NOTE BOOK · Ref.139 · Punched for filing

6

Writing about others: our other selves

So, you've found your story, and you've found your voice. You're able to switch off the critical wittering that taunts you, whispering that it is not your story to tell, and who cares anyway? Or worse, the voices that tell you that you can't do it – you don't have a right, or you're not good enough. But these stories are so important to you, and so persistent. They follow you around, asking to be better understood; sometimes you wonder if it is even a choice. You sit down and start to write. But then you mention it to your family ...

There are many questions you'll be asked on the rocky road to trying to write memoir and personal narrative, particularly by non-writers, or those who don't write and don't understand why you would put your private life out there for all to read (they probably don't read memoir, much, either). Here, in my attempt to prepare you, I will answer some of those questions. But, like most other big events of your life (giving birth, buying a house, going through a divorce), it's impossible to imagine what it will be like until you do it, and the experience will be different for everyone. To get as broad a view as is possible, I have drawn on my writer interviews. I have come to believe that every writer of memoir should have an ethical code of practice, one that reminds them of their moral standards, those things that matter to them, and that they can refer back to when challenged. I am hoping that by the end of this chapter, you'll be a little closer to forming yours.

Why write memoir when you could write fiction?

There is a simple answer to this question – read this book! But I guess if you're this far, you have read it, or maybe you are so hung up on the issues around ethics and the fear of hurting those you love by exposing family secrets, you have skipped straight to this chapter and won't bother with the rest. I do, obviously, urge you to read the other chapters, for the very real and important reasons why memoir matters, not just for those writing it, but also for their families and for those reading it. It is so powerful and necessary to stand by an experience and say, hand on heart, *this is my truth*, particularly when there are experiences that have impacted your life, followed you around, 'something shapeless which suffuses my whole body and interrupts me when I try to speak, with a voice only I can hear', as Masud so elegantly expressed it.

And what if, by writing this story, you might bring loved ones into the fold because you've found a way of expressing what might have felt ineffable? It might even shift the narrative and open opportunity for you and your family to talk in a way that wasn't possible before. What if it also helps readers face difficult, obstructive feelings in themselves? It might change their perspective, and give them a new language, shining a light on their life and how they have previously lived, and asking for them to consider it differently. Memoir is direct. In your face. It is unapologetic. It can also be a conversation starter. It is a real-life story, a real person who felt the heat of experience, the rush of joy and the flood of tears. Of course, fiction can be honest too, but fiction tends to wear a mask.

Many years ago, I went to a talk by a successful female writer – one who is famous for drawing on her life when writing fiction – and she was asked a question by a member of the audience: what makes you decide to write something as fiction as opposed to memoir? One part of her answer really stuck with me: if she is ashamed of an experience she will write it as fiction, because she can hide behind fiction, it offered her a cloak as disguise. This comment has returned to me over the years. Of course, implicit in this answer are different types of shame. You might feel shame for something that has happened to you, beyond your control: call it abuse, or violence imposed on you by others. This might be an internalised shame, in you as the victim of the abuse, particularly if you have been forced by the abuser or the culture around you to stay silent, and particularly if it happened when you were a child. I don't know if the writer was referring to this kind of shame, but I wonder if I felt disturbed by her answer because if you bury your shame in fiction, aren't you joining the cultural silence that made you feel that way in the first place? Do you not continue and condone this legacy?

I am drawn to the psychotherapist Sándor Ferenczi's definition of trauma, as expressed in his clinical diary published in 1932, as 'the unforeseen, the unfathomable, the incalculable ...' due to an 'unexpected, external threat, the sense of which one cannot grasp, is unbearable'. Trauma happens without warning, which leaves the person to whom it happens unprepared and undefended. After the trauma, according to Ferenczi, one's trust in the benevolence of the external world is destroyed and one feels betrayed. But the traumatic experience that Ferenczi found the most destructive was emotional abandonment from the parent – the child being alone with no one to turn to. One variant of this abandonment is the parent's lack of understanding or, worse, their denial that the traumatic event happened. The lasting effects of trauma result from the absence of a kind, understanding environment, 'Traumatic aloneness ... is what really renders the attack traumatic, that is, causing the psyche to crack'.

Whether you're writing fiction or non-fiction, writing through trauma helps you bear witness to your own experience; and putting it out into the world opens the experience to your readers to do the same. But memoir is more direct. Jade Angeles Fitton, speaking of writing her memoir, *Hermit*, told me how her memoir has been a kind of spokesperson for her, a safe space where she could express parts of herself she wasn't able to otherwise. The page is a contained space, and the act of writing is private and intimate, and allows a writer to enter the well of their psychic and emotional world. The page also in many ways is a safe place, because once written and published it is more removed than if it was spoken: my reader can sit alone in their living room or bedroom and read and react to my words, while I remain in the safety of my home. I only need to hear about it later if I choose to (and if they have felt moved enough to reach out).

I was struck by the many readers who offered sympathy for what I had shared in my memoir, because perhaps I didn't think what had happened to me was that bad; after all, it had been my reality. Readers' responses gave me acknowledgement, which helped me stop identifying so closely with those aspects of my past that had caused me harm, which had become ingrained in my behaviour and belief about myself. This release can be very powerful and liberating. The shame, as #MeToo has taught us, does not belong to you, but belongs to the abuser, or the culture which has enabled it, and so part of healing is placing the shame back where it belongs. If you write through your shame, and come to understand it better, and then share that understanding with the world, you might help liberate others to do the same.

In our conversation, Damian Barr told me how each of the books he has written has found its form. He was offered a deal to write *Maggie & Me* as a novel, but, he says, 'I wanted to tell the truth – and be seen as telling the truth – because I was told so often as a child nobody would believe me, and I should be ashamed. So for me, the act of telling and witnessing my own life was reparative.'

Vanessa Springora spoke with me about her extraordinary memoir, *Le Consentement* (Consent), which exposes a long-term predatory sexual relationship she had when she was just turning 14 with a famous French writer, Gabriel Matzneff, who was about 50 at the time. Springora told me that she had been carrying the book inside her for years, but was too afraid of the repercussions both personally and professionally if she wrote it as non-fiction, and so instead she initially wrote it as fiction, 'a kind of rewrite of Nabokov's *Lolita*, but from the victim's point of view,' she tells me, but it was 'a more romanticised version that didn't satisfy me at all'. She goes on to say this version was far too distanced and too far from reality. But then various events aligned to propel her to return to it – her stepson and daughter became teenagers and, observing them, she began to fully understand the teenage sensibility: 'I saw they were still big children, naive, sensitive and vulnerable. Which makes them ideal prey.' Also, there was a news item in France that involved an 11-year-old girl who had been abused by an adult, and her mother had filed a complaint for rape, but even though there had been penetration, the rape was requalified as sexual assault because the child was supposedly 'consenting'. 'I told myself that this concept of "consent" only served to clear the criminals, never to protect the victims.'

Another trigger was that, in 2013, Matzneff was awarded the Prix Renaudot, a major French literary prize, without arousing the slightest indignation in the publishing world in which Springora worked. 'I saw it as a kind of denial, which I felt was both bruising and provocative.' Springora feared nothing had changed since the 1980s, when the abuse had happened. As we will explore below, Springora's memoir, which was published in 2020, landed at a crucial time and had huge influence on the consent laws and the way the public viewed intergenerational sexual relations between adult and child.

But what if the shame does belong to you? What if you have done something shameful that you don't want to admit to in such an undisguised way? My answer is this: shame breeds in secrecy and silence. What if you lift the lid on that shame and expose it for all to see, and you discover it is not as shameful as you had first perceived?

Or, better still, your readers are grateful to you for sharing such a profound truth, and begin to open up and admit to their own shameful experiences? A conversation ensues. Maybe it is not so much the act itself, but it is the way it is perceived. A bit of examination and analysis reveals the limitations of a society that has an insidious hold on its members in its attempts to remain in control. I often return to 'The Love of My Life', a courageous and powerful essay by the author Cheryl Strayed, about how in her despair after her mother's death she goes on a sexual rampage with strangers, married and grieving.

> It was only a kiss, and barely that, but it was, anyway, a crossing. When I was a child I witnessed a leaf unfurl in a single motion. One second it was a fist, the next an open hand. I never forgot it, seeing so much happen so fast. And this was like that – the end of one thing, the beginning of another: my life as a slut.

It was published in *The Sun* magazine in 2002 and continues to be the most visited article on its website, not so much because of the sex – although I am sure the sex is part of it – but more because the essay's power is in its wisdom, and willingness to be bare to the bone, and courageous in the face of exposure. It sheds an unwavering light on the phenomenon of having a heightened sexuality in grief, and the open (and in 2002 certainly not so common) admission that women, too, pursue sex devoid of emotion.

In many ways, the sex is a conduit, a way for a woman to act out a grief that has overwhelmed her. And it is so much more effective here in essay form than if Strayed had hidden herself behind a surrogate character or set of situations in fiction. In an introduction to the essay, celebrating *The Sun's* fiftieth year in print, the assistant editor, Staci Kleinmaier, writes: 'I can hardly believe there was a moment when I thought the written word couldn't help people. Writing – the kind that shows the heartache and beauty of this world, writing like Strayed's – is one of life's richest gifts. It saved me.'

I often tell my students that we should listen to the resistances, and look into the cracks, those areas we would rather leave hidden. It is those places that we perceive as the darkest that hold the most energy, and, when we look hard enough, they begin to let the light in. Be sure to have support around you, but trust the process. Sometimes we have to tolerate discomfort to come through (slightly altered) the other side.

Okay, fair enough. You might want to work through stuff on the page. But (surely?) you'd never think of publishing?

[And] The book gets relegated again to the bottom drawer. Or, it doesn't ...

There are many reasons to write memoir. You might want to write it for yourself as a type of testimony to past experience, or as a gift to a mother or father, or your children, future generations, a record of a life, bringing together letters and diaries and artefacts. Maybe your aim is to self-publish and distribute among those same family members; you don't have ambitions to publish to the mainstream. Or, maybe you do. You have a message to impart beyond a series of memories or happenings, and the story feels more relevant, more urgent, than if it was just a few readers. There is something revealed about the world in which we live that might offer a new perspective, and it might educate or illuminate in such a way that is original or refreshing.

In most cases, you won't know at the start of writing a memoir if it will have a wider vision and appeal – finding an audience beyond simply yourself or those closest to you – but you are propelled back to the page, and the more time you spend at the keyboard, crafting words, reading, researching, questions opening up, the more invested you become. Before you know it, the book is written, and your closest readers – be they your family or friends or a writer's group – tell you there is something special here, something that speaks to them. You land an agent, you land a publishing deal.

I was confronted with this question when I published *Sins of My Father*: 'It's fine to write it, but why put it out in the world for all to read?' And I get it. It is an invasion of people's privacy, to have these important and often painful experiences given form and made indelible for any stranger to read.

An important part of writing memoir is the harnessing of courage and strength enough to take a risk. But it's also about asking difficult questions of the self. Why am I writing this? Is it important beyond my need to find words to articulate experience? Is the subject bigger than those whom it might hurt? Can I stand by this book in the public eye and defend my reasons for writing it? I find it helpful when I am dreaming up a new idea to imagine it published, and project forwards to a bookshop event, an audience in front of me, a Q&A. When publishing fiction, the interviewer and audience might focus on the writerly technique – the craft of how the book is written

– but with memoir the interviewer will inevitably probe into the life from which it has sprung.

Ask yourself, how would you feel answering questions in public about your life? Are you okay with articulating painful episodes from the recent past that might make you look uncomfortable or compromised or expose moral shortfalls? What happens if you clam up? Or get defensive of yourself or those you love. Are you ready emotionally to stand up in a crowded room and defend what you have done? What if you find yourself triggered; what if you cry? If I was to write about my divorce, for instance, I would have to be okay answering personal questions about my domestic life, and an experience that had far-reaching consequences, for my children and those I love. (I write more about the pitfalls of writing about children below.)

But publishing memoir can have a ripple effect that can go on to change many lives. Vanessa Springora's memoir, *Le Consentement*, sparked, as reported in the *Guardian*, 'an international furore': it was translated in over thirty countries and adapted for stage and the cinema (the film *Consent* was released in 2023) and helped change the consent laws in France, as well as leading to Matzneff's exposure and his being sued for 'glorification of paedophilia'. In discussion with me, Springora said: 'writing this book has above all enabled me to right an injustice. On an individual level, it enabled me to tell my truth, to put forward a counter-narrative that opposed the idyllic version Matzneff gave in his books of the abuse he inflicted on his victims, and on me.' It started as a personal form of justice, which enabled Springora to have some power when she wasn't able to lodge a legal complaint about the abuse retroactively due to France's statute of limitations.

Since Matzneff had overwritten part of Springora's history by immortalising her and other schoolgirls in his books, it was only right that she reclaim that history as her own, in her own book with her own words. 'To restore a piece of truth, my own,' she says. 'From a symbolic point of view, it was very important for me to be heard, to be read, to be believed and to be understood. And to feel alone no longer.'

Springora's is a clear example of the potential impact of a memoir being widely read through mainstream publication and beyond. And when I am questioned about why I took the decision to make public an aspect of my family's private life, I find Springora's case an inspiration. I also remind myself of the ripple effect of my own memoir. I had been struck when watching *Wild Wild Country*, the bestselling Netflix documentary about the Rajneesh cult of which my father was a disciple, that there was no mention of the effect the movement had on the families who joined and were left, and the children, many of whom followed their parents to the communes. During the pandemic I met online with the Dutch filmmaker Maroesja Perizonius, who herself had grown up in the communes and made a film about it, *Communekind* (*Child of the Commune*). Together we pitched and developed a documentary, *Children of the Cult*, which would remedy this omission. After a couple of years of perseverance, we finally found a production team that understood our vision, and an ITV commission followed. The film had a nationwide cinema release in 2024 and widespread publicity with interviews in all the major UK newspapers, along with five-star reviews. It was also nominated for a BAFTA. But most importantly, it gave a platform for women and men who had been abused and neglected growing up within the Osho community, and the publicity helped bolster a class-action case against the Osho International Foundation organisation. My memoir was part of a conversation, a building of momentum among a generation of people whose voice had been subsumed by those of their parents and the spiritual movement they were involved in.

I didn't know at the time of writing *Sins of My Father* that its publication might influence this outcome – how could I? – but I did follow a hunch that the neglect and abuse that had happened to me when I was on holiday in my father's commune was part of a bigger and more horrific picture. In fact, this systemic abuse and neglect had become a 'dirty little secret' that everyone knew but no one spoke of. Does this outcome justify the pain it caused to some of those people who didn't want me to publish it? It is not for me to say, but it would be terrible if *Children of the Cult* had not been made, and those survivors had not had a chance to tell their stories. A memoir might be simply a catalyst, but a catalyst is essential for change.

Okay, so the answer is yes – and you are determined to publish. How do you protect yourself in the process?

The author Susanna Crossman spoke to me about forming her own 'architectural blueprint' before she had even started writing her memoir *Home Is Where We Start*, about growing up in a utopian Marxist community in the 1970s and 1980s. 'I reflected about the "how", "what" and "why", and which doors I wanted to open.' This is her own ethical code of practice in many ways, because it gives her some control over the text from the very beginning, aware as she is of her intention.

Other writers want the freedom to write unimpeded, particularly when writing the first draft. Melissa Febos, author of a memoir (*Whip Smart*) and two essay collections, and *Body Work*, her own craft book on the radical power of writing personal narrative, told me that at the start of a new book she makes a promise to herself never to show what she is writing to anyone. It is what gives her permission to write into painful and challenging experience (*Whip Smart* is about Febos's time as a professional dominatrix). 'The alchemy is that by the time it is finished the writing process has released me from the shame,' she tells me. As I've demonstrated in other chapters throughout this book, I too believe that the degrees of separation from the first flush of raw expression to the finished product can bring insurmountable transformation in oneself and one's relationship with the past. Most books take years to write, and another year or so before they are published.

But with decades of experience of psychiatric work as an arts therapist, Crossman believes that there are realms of intimacy and trauma that are difficult to enter, and sometimes it is better to remain outside of these. There is a paradox then for the writer because they also must recall an experience viscerally to render it effective for the reader. A writer of memoir also doesn't want to appear to be self-censoring or withholding.

Clare Best, who writes about the buried memory of incest sexual abuse in her memoir, *The Missing List*, spoke to me about how she 'particularly struggled with how to write the scenes of abuse – I wanted to avoid writing them at all, but that would have felt like a form of denial and dissociation, and I had already lived that way for decades.' In the end, despite having written many more passages that didn't make it into the book, she included only two or three brief scenes that are directly about abuse. There is a lot of skill in writing sparely and writing it well, and when this involves traumatic events it can be surprisingly powerful, because, between the lines, the reader can feel the subtle dance the author makes between her necessary self-protection and the importance of the silence finally being broken. What is not stated flowers in the imagination.

But Best also felt the need to be upfront and honest about the cold and dark reality of her experience, and so adds what she names a 'List of Charges Against My Father' in the Afterword. It is stark and distressing reading, rightfully presented as bullet points, with no attempt to dress it up in poetic prose. In the Afterword, Best reflects on the importance of this decision despite how difficult it was for her: 'The List of Charges has made me feel so intensely uncomfortable, and so unwilling to cause discomfort in others, that I almost decided to exclude it. In the end, I am including it precisely because of that discomfort.'

Best says that to write the most difficult sections, she needed to feel 'strong enough, but also vulnerable enough ... Often, I would write the toughest passages when I had just come home from a therapy session and could still feel acutely the safety and support of that therapy room, together with its courage, honesty and acceptance.'

Ali Millar told me she really did not enjoy writing the first draft of *The Last Days* at all. She would be sick, have panic attacks, would need to wash. 'I never showered as much as I did that summer.' But writing the first draft quickly became a kind of protection for Millar, as it enabled her to get it all out, to find its shape, however messy, and then to return to it later to redraft. She describes re-entering the past as 'communing with the dead ... sometimes I'd wake up and not know which bedroom I was in'. When writing subsequent drafts, Millar often played music as a way to get back into scenes – 'Songs helped me enter experience at a granular level, what I was seeing, smelling and hearing.'

Crossman told me she made sure to give herself treats while she was writing her memoir: 'These included trawling second-hand clothes websites, sea-swimming, coffee, wine and a little trash TV (Chinese romance movies and Christmas movies).' The author Catherine Taylor told me that when writing *The Stirrings: A Memoir in Northern Time*, about growing up in Sheffield amidst the haunting threat of nuclear war and the Yorkshire Ripper, 'I went for lots of walks ... Much tea was drunk. Did I mention my love of Ritz crackers?'

Taylor also warns: 'you should never publish what you don't want anyone to read. I thought a lot about that, and about how memoir is only a fraction of one's life, and not all of it, and no one is entitled to know everything about you just because you've chosen to share some aspects.'

We are also protected by the fact that all writing is performative. The moment we put words to a piece of paper, they become something other than the experience they describe, and the story takes hold. Even more so if we have created something artful, something that transcends the experience we are writing about. 'As a writer, our main aim is to illuminate a human experience that is legible,' says Melissa Febos. The plot, the narrative tension, it all helps with the necessary distance.

There is a big difference between a journalistic exposé and a memoir which has the space and breadth to go deep into its subject and ask questions of it. Good memoir tests and challenges what is known; it plays with language, questions the single interpretation. Are you writing a victim narrative? Then question yourself – complicate the concept of victim narratives and ask, as the author and journalist Leah McLaren did in her memoir, *Where You End and I Begin*, aren't we all victims? Haven't we all been mistreated somewhere along the line? And what good is it to think of yourself a victim? Nothing is black and white within the pages of a memoir – or it shouldn't be. Every anecdote is deepened, every statement questioned for its truth and validity. We don't have all the answers, and the book we write should reflect this. All we can do is inspire curiosity.

As I write this, we occupy a precarious and divisive space where, post #MeToo, the general mood is to bare all and speak of personal experience, however transgressive. But in the internet age, there is also an appetite for public disgrace and the seemingly inexhaustible supply of vitriol and simple cruelty among many who wish to inflict pain and shame on those who put their heads above the parapet. Within this climate, it feels even more important for those writing memoir, and mining personal, often traumatic experience, to think and think again about how much they want their personal story to be in the public eye and for what purpose.

What if our biggest protector in writing memoir is the craft itself? We are not putting our journals out there for all to read, and we're not recalling scenes for the sake of simply recalling detail, event or anecdote. All this should be in service to meaning, or a message or theme that a writer is exploring. As you will have read in the chapter on 'Radical deconstruction', there are many ways of writing around a subject, or going deeper than the events themselves, finding image and metaphor to present experience, and responding to greater cultural questions.

As a means of using art as self-protection, Rachel Cusk's memoir *Aftermath*, about the fraught weeks after her separation from her husband, is infused with metaphor. She uses a tooth extraction as a diversion from having to write onerous painful detail about the day her husband moves out of the house. 'The day my husband moved his possessions out of our house I had toothache ... I stood at the bottom of the stairs, my hands over my mouth, like a mime artist pantomiming dismay.' As if the tooth – which had grown at an angle – stands in for the narrator, she writes: 'Why had it assumed that shape? It was difficult to know, the dentist said. It may have been bent by the pressure of other forces, but there appeared to be an aspect of fate to it too, the response of its own nature to the available conditions.' She goes on to write: 'the tooth itself would have to answer for its doomed character. It had been in some ineluctable sense wayward, and now it had put itself beyond reach ... that which is shaped and therefore shapes its own fate.' Between these pages, Cusk is both oblique and transparent. Her writing has a maturity about it, an emotional preparedness to be what Phillip

Lopate refers to as a generosity to be 'honest and open to exposure', despite it not being literal. Buried in its artfulness is a searing truth. We know very little about the individuals involved and much more about the emotions explored, but through a third dimension.

In my own case, instead of focusing solely on the particulars of my marriage breakup, I might look more broadly at the phenomenon that affects almost half of the married population: what it means to a couple to want to break up, what it means to that family – and more widely to a culture. The death of the promise of a lifelong union. The death of the fairy tale. I might, as the American author Lyz Lenz has done with her bestselling 2024 memoir, *This American Ex-Wife*, try to reframe the narrative around divorce from one of deficiency to one of freedom, being able to advocate for yourself, and even flourish. Leslie Jamison's *Splinters* similarly confronts and flips the divorce narrative and that of single motherhood, but in poetic form and prose. In a *Vogue* interview Jamison speaks of how she was interested in writing whittled pieces that build something expansive, and that the difference between what might be a raw outpouring and cooked prose is revision, as a kind of 're-visioning', stepping back and seeing the three-dimensional view. 'My goal is always to bring that retrospective vision into some kind of synthesis with the lush particularity that comes from drafting closer to experience. It's like introspective bifocals: you see things from far away and close-up at once.' Lenz speaks of the importance of memoirs that challenge the status quo, particularly since in the US, despite most divorces being initiated by women (around 70 per cent), there is still stigma around a woman, particularly a mother, who leaves. Memoirs like hers and Jamison's help find a language for what is becoming a societal phenomenon before society has caught up on itself.

What if I also want to write about the first flush of falling in love after divorce? Rather than getting bogged down by the everyday details, I think of our relationship within a more deeply existential context: how important it was when we first met for me to *believe* in something, and how this need to believe came out of the therapy sessions I was having, and back further to the relationship I had with my midwife when I was pregnant with my first child. If my story is about *belief*, rather than simply love, I have a framework, a place from which to write it – the therapist's couch, for instance – and the story has a reason for being that reaches beyond the simple details of a life. It becomes an exploration of an idea, and that exploration gives the story purpose, a reason to explore love, and a drive, a quest to answer questions, which in turn gives the story forward momentum. Craft then acts as a protective framework for the tender stuff of personal experience. It gives what can otherwise feel subjective and ephemeral some necessary authority, breadth and gravity.

With your commitment to the craft of memoir and to shaping memory comes the need to really get to know your content. When I teach memoir, I encourage my students to constantly check in with themselves, not simply about how best to write a particular scene, but also about what impact they are chasing, and how much they can expose about their lives and still feel comfortable. These questions and decisions all go towards building a personal and strong relationship with your content and coming to learn your own moral and ethical standard, so when it comes to the work being published you can stand by it as *your* story, *your* version of events, thought through and considered. This building of confidence in *your* voice and *your* story will also help with your sense of autonomy, and your right to write this story.

If you are committing experience to the page too soon then you are too close to the events and the feelings; if the wound is too raw, if it has not yet scabbed over, then wait. Write, edit, read, think, craft and form. Write poetry, write fiction, write something profoundly academic. Be open and surrender to the process. But above all, as Febos says, write that first draft for yourself, because it is only then that you will engage with your true voice, and do it justice. And when you come to having to defend your words – because you will have to – you will know that you did the best you could because you wrote honestly and truthfully about what you remember, and what matters.

In my teaching, I often quote the author Julia Bell who once said to me that you should take your time over a book, particularly if it's very personal, and it's all in the quality of the gaze. This reminds me of a Phillip Lopate quote: 'Try to write as beautifully as possible, because well-wrought prose invites its own forgiveness – from you yourself, if not from the offended party.'

But what about your loved ones? They never asked to be written into your memoir

I used to say that everyone is entitled to their story. It's your story to tell. But I don't say this any longer, because no one is an island, and it is inevitable that your story will merge with others', be it your sister, your brother, your parents, your cousins. Firstly, acknowledgement is needed. Yes, I hear you. This is a valid worry. This worry comes from a deep place of compassion, respect for others, and fear. And it has grounding, because in teaching memoir for the past ten years, I have heard a few horror stories of relatives hurt, and families shattered. But only a few … and in most cases this hasn't happened. Or if it has, the damage has been brief, and has forced conversations that might not have happened otherwise; relationships have been pushed into new, and often better, shapes. New trust and depth of understanding comes into being.

It is worth stating the obvious: that memoir is subjective, and therefore cannot be understood as the empirical truth. Yeah, yeah, heard that, you might think, but writers and their families get into real trouble by not grasping this simple fact. I elaborate by adding: the recollection of past events is highly personal and often driven by a strong emotion, which can make it faulty, factually suspect and fallible. Memoir is a very odd specimen because it is by its nature based on a kind of truth and categorised as non-fiction, but it is also, above all else, a story. And because it is driven by emotion, it is often flammable and volatile. Which of course makes it problematic in its nature, both morally and ethically, for ourselves but also for others. Whichever way you look at it, and however careful you might be, writing memoir invades a loved one's privacy, which will feel uncomfortable for many, and at worst will cause pain.

In her spirited book *The Art of Memoir*, Mary Karr spells out a very useful ethical code, and she briefly pins it down to three stages. She will notify anyone who features in her memoir way in advance, 'to give them a chance to shoot it down'; once she's started writing, she keeps the pages to herself; and when finished she sends the manuscript to those relevant people with enough time before publication. In discussion with me, Melissa Febos says: 'my ethical code has evolved with every book. Do I have an ongoing relationship with that person? Have I scrutinised my behaviour more than I have theirs? Because I have written about abusive past partners who have been enraged, I am okay if I stick to my code.' In an attempt to start thinking about what our own ethical code might be, I thought it would be useful to list some tips from the writers I've spoken to, to see how they navigate this sticky question of protecting themselves and those they love. By doing this, I also reflect on my own.

When writing *A Flat Place*, Noreen Masud 'made a decision that I wasn't going to write in detail about living people whom I didn't love, or where there was too much active pain to be just to them. So I could write about my father, who is dead and whom I didn't love, and I could write about my mother, who is alive but whom I love.' I relate to this stance, as it points to what I keep returning to in this book – the importance of emotional distance. This includes emotional distance from those people who have affected our lives, or upset us in some way. It's fine to 'write angry', but not advised to publish a memoir that includes unprocessed pain or grief, and writing for revenge should always be avoided. Ideally, when we do share our manuscript with those who feature in it, we want what we have written to be accepted. Even if our loved ones are upset by what they have read, we hope they feel it has its place, that it has been considered. Masud didn't give her mother veto over the text, but did ask her to flag whatever she wasn't happy with – 'I emphasised that I might not be able to make all the changes she requested, but that I would do my best to make responsive edits as far as I possibly could.' In the end Masud's mother made only one change: 'I had noted that she converted to Islam when she married my father, and she asked me to add the word 'officially' – she had *officially* converted.' Masud continues to tell me that other parts of the memoir caused her mother pain, 'but she didn't ask me to change them'. This one simple change, the addition of a word, and its importance to Masud's mother reveals another layer of meaning.

Jade Angeles Fitton spoke about a 'duty of love' towards her family members, and how this involved caution when it came to exposing them to the more challenging aspects of her past written about in her memoir, *Hermit*. Sometimes this duty of love involves you as a writer taking responsibility for the pain of others. But Fitton also spoke of the importance of discretion: 'I think the greatest display of love a writer can show is to keep other people's secrets. To not even disguise them through fiction. Some things are sacred and, in my opinion, there are places you just don't go.'

Kit de Waal had a unique way of approaching writing her memoir, *Without Warning and Only Sometimes*. She spoke to me about it as a 'communal story', and said she wouldn't have written it if she hadn't had her siblings' consent. She also gave her siblings power of veto over everything. 'If one of my brothers or sisters said I don't like that, or that didn't happen, it would have come out,' she tells me. When she sent them the manuscript she said in her email: 'Here it is, this is what is going to be published, you have the power of veto over any chapter, scene, line or word – if you don't like it, it comes out.' 'It's their history,' she says, 'and what I am fine with being out in the world is not necessarily what they are happy with being out in the world.' Paradoxically, Susanna Crossman had a different way of dealing with the collective experience. Having grown up in a Marxist community, her biggest challenge in writing her memoir, *Home Is Where We Start*, was shaking off that collective psychology in order to claim the story as her own.

Like De Waal, Anna Wilson offered her husband and siblings veto when reading the manuscript of her memoir about her mother's late diagnosis of autism, *A Place for Everything*. However, she says she offered this only because she was fairly confident they would be okay with the text as they'd read it already in blog form, and had encouraged her to adapt her blog posts for memoir. I also found it helpful to publish personal essays prior to publishing *Sins of My Father*, to acclimatise myself to having my personal story in the public eye, as much as to get my family used to the idea as well.

In contrast, Marina Benjamin feels that the author should not give others veto on what should be included. She stresses it is entirely the writer's responsibility, and she doesn't think it's right to expect family members to make that decision for them. 'I think it's my job to exercise due diligence when it comes to writing about others, to listen to any cavil family members may entertain. My job to make the judgement call on what can be said and what can't. I suspect other writers won't agree with me on this, but it's my long-considered take.' Like Benjamin, Catherine

Taylor is clear that the story is her own, and that no one should have veto. The only person who saw *The Stirrings* before press was her editor.

There are many memoirs that leave out particular family members entirely. Taylor wrote about siblings and parents very remotely, to protect them but also because she was quite a solitary child and so her memories often involved her being alone. And Clare Best similarly held back from writing too much about her brothers, because she felt they had their own perspectives and therefore their own stories.

Richard Beard has an interesting angle on the question of whether or not to show the manuscript to loved ones. While he didn't feel he needed permission to write his memoir, *The Day That Went Missing*, because the story of his brother's drowning, he felt, was primarily his story (he was in the water when it happened), he did want to get his family involved, and 'The best way to get a family involved is to talk to them, interview them and make them a part of the story'. He brings these conversations alive in the text and charts the frustrating but urgent journey his family and he go on from denial to acceptance, weaving between present and past, particularly when speaking to his mother who had created a fiction in her attempt to live with the reality of his brother's drowning. She had not remembered Beard being in the water with his brother when he died. 'The passing of time has eroded the truth, and over the years Mum has lifted me from the water and placed me safely in her care on the beach, all her precious boys present and correct except Nicky.' But through Beard's persistent questioning and collection of evidence from every which way he looks, the cloak of denial slowly lifts. '"Only hope it was over quickly," Mum says, thinking of Nicky in the water because the day and the boy and the death are newly open for discussion. Their time has come again.' Which leads Beard to return to the beach where it happened, 'seeking out raw feeling, of the type I've denied for so long'.

Tom Lee told me of his regret that he wasn't able to involve his parents more while writing his memoir, *The Bullet*, about his and his family's periods of mental illness. During the time it took for Lee to write his memoir, his father died and his mother retreated into depression. 'In many ways, I would like the book to have been much more collaborative,' he told me. 'If my mother had been younger and fitter and if my dad hadn't died I could have involved them more, because one of the things I still don't know, or don't understand, quite possibly never will, is quite what my mother's illness was like for her. And in a sense, that's one of the most interesting things to me. Her voice isn't really in the book too much, which is a shame.'

I agree that inviting family to get involved can help in many ways: it gives them investment in the project but it also supports the story with various viewpoints, brings their voices into the narrative, and deepens and expands the story. I had to ask my mother to tell me stories about her childhood, how her family had emigrated from South Africa to Wiltshire and started a farm, and how she and her seven siblings ran wild, left alone to explore the countryside, setting fire to hay bales, and running barefoot, much to their neighbours' shock. I still look back with affection to those sessions we spent together around her kitchen table, while she recalled intimate stories of her and my father and how they met and got married, how they set up home and worked side by side at a makeshift desk, she writing biographies and he running a publishing business from a back bedroom in our house. I threaded in her voice from those conversations, reflecting on the past, and what it had come to mean to her.

Asking my mother now, four years later, to reflect on what it felt like to read my memoir in draft form, she says she came to understand me and my suffering better, which felt particularly important for healing the wounds that were inflicted between us when I suddenly left my marriage (and she was furious with me). 'It is always shocking at first,' she says. 'You think you know your children, but to read their pain and anguish as well as joy is essential for realising they are a formed human being, independent from you and your idea of them.' When I sent my mum my manuscript before it went into publication, I told her firmly that there was no need to edit. It was still to go to the copyeditor. But, being a writer, she couldn't help herself. I never forget her handing back my manuscript with multiple red lines struck through it, old style. I thanked her, but also felt it was important to say – as Masud had with her own mother – I will pay attention to all your suggestions, but won't be able to make all the changes you requested. It was essential that my memoir was my voice and my story.

My mother and I watched our relationship evolve and we emerged from the memoir-writing process closer, two women, side by side. Jade Angeles Fitton speaks of how her sister came to understand her better after she read her memoir. 'Because I am not a "talker" sometimes people think I am shutting them out. It's been a difficult thing, but also a good thing for people I love. It's opened up conversations.' She was nervous about her husband's parents seeing a different version of her through *Hermit*, but when they became 'cheerleaders of the book', she felt accepted: not just a part of her, which had felt limited and even fraudulent, but all of her.

For Masud, also, her mother's reading of her memoir brought with it emotional resolution: 'She wrote back to me saying that she didn't remember everything I had written about, but she was so sorry that there had been so much pain. What a perfect response. I feel much closer to her now – I was aching to hear that, I think.' Writing *A Flat Place* was a chance for Masud to make her feelings understood. There is something very intimate about this – about someone close to you reading you in words, a world of your making, symbols created and explored as a way of articulating an otherwise ungraspable interior landscape.

But sending your manuscript to family members or loved ones does not necessarily mean it will be read. You might offer it to them to read, particularly if they feature in it, or the story is close to the bone, but they can choose to say no. This might also extend to when the book is published and out there in the world. I was initially hurt that some of my aunts chose not to read my memoir, despite knowing why. It hadn't been their choice to dredge up the past, presented for all to see. They didn't want to remember, and I had no right to put them through that just because I had made the choice to revisit it again. I also realised that I had processed so much of the emotion through the act of writing itself. I had lived and breathed it for many years. Whereas for them, here was a fully formed (and subjective) story thrust into their hands.

Editing and taking time over the text gives you detachment, and distance gives you time to reflect. Dr Tulika Jha, who was still writing her memoir when we had our discussion, said, 'Had the relationships been easy to navigate, I would not be working through these issues via writing a memoir, I would have worked through them with my loved ones!' But what might have angered you at a certain point in the writing process has a chance, through writing, to transform into compassion. Speaking to me of writing her memoir in poems, *Hymnal*, Julia Bell told me that taking her time also allowed her to have emotional distance. From the final draft, she withdrew the angrier poems and also injected some humour, which her readers appreciated. The writer and broadcaster Mike Parker writes in the *Wales Arts Review*: 'Religious fundamentalism, national identity, class, sickly family dynamics and homophobia are all difficult topics that can easily overwhelm fine writing, but Bell dances past the pitfalls with such grace and style, without ever cheapening their reality. Her wit is sharp and ever-present, but make no mistake, she is deadly serious.'

Technique and skill are good defences when tackling the sticky problem of writing about loved ones. Writing memoir doesn't stop us from disguising characters: for instance, we can change their names, or omit names altogether. But metaphor also acts as a good diversion, a roundabout way of exploring difficult emotion. As we saw above, Rachel Cusk does this well in *Aftermath*, her memoir about her divorce: rather than exposing the dramas of what is happening, she focuses on the everyday remains, 'scraping at the marrow of experience' the 'small authentic thing over the big inflated thing'. The dishwasher breaks, the drains clog, the knobs of cupboards and doors come away unrepentantly in the hand.

Despite Clover Stroud's third memoir, *The Red of My Blood*, being about her sister's premature death from cancer and Stroud's immediate and visceral response, she didn't want to write the moment of her sister's death, for obvious reasons of privacy, but also because 'as a reader, you don't need to be taken to that place'. Stroud tells me: 'I've always felt as though I'm writing right into the heart of it, but that doesn't mean writing the whole of it.'

Similarly, when writing about the traumatic memory of her father's violence in her *Granta* essay, 'Personal Growth', Marina Benjamin creates her own limitations. She challenged herself not to use the word 'trauma' and to keep descriptions of the violence to a bare minimum – she would write about 'high temperature' material in a 'low temperature' way. Less is certainly more, as the scenes of violence are written plainly and with detachment, and in some cases even humorously – 'like a cartoon character spitting heat, to redden and swell, sending him jumping to his feet with his arms windmilling madly, going slap, slap, slap at my face'. Benjamin then diverts the narrative by drawing away from the drama and nodding to the unreliable nature of memory – 'there's only a jump cut, and then I'm under the bed in the dark ...'.

Memoir and personal narrative often marry scene-setting and reflection, which allows the writer to zoom in and out, to go in for the detail, and draw out to a wider view, almost like a camera focusing in through a window after panning across a landscape. The wider view might explore a theme through referencing poetry or literature, bringing in scientific research or statistics to offer gravity to the experience presented. In the case of Benjamin's essay, in her understanding of herself as a child refusing to eat, one of the greater themes is refusal. In the context of the power dynamics within her family she concludes: 'refusal is the last recourse of the powerless, and it can be wielded to good effect'. Refusal becomes a weapon for the young Benjamin, but it also allows the essay to divert on to the solid, unemotional ground of quoting research, expanding out into the universal and providing an educational respite for the writer from difficult and personal material, and therefore also for the reader, who can take an out breath, while learning something.

But there are, of course, cases when writing memoir causes such a deep fissure in a family that recovery might feel impossible. The journalist and author Leah McLaren took the usual precautions before publishing her memoir, *Where You End and I Begin*, by sending proofs to those who were mentioned in the text, which were signed off. But when it came to publication, her childhood best friend, who features briefly but significantly in the book, published a blog post on the social media platform Medium about how McLaren had misrepresented her and an incident between them at a pool party when they were teenagers. McLaren's mother was also disappointed with her for exposing an abusive relationship of her own that she had experienced as a young teenager, despite having previously given her consent to the mention. The book had started as a collaboration between her and her mother, but the parameters changed as the story progressed into being less about McLaren's mother and more about her own childhood.

'In a work of rigorous journalism you double and triple check your sources,' McLaren says in conversation with me. 'As you're trying to get as close as you possibly can to the empirical truth – in memoir it's different: your subjective truth has great value, but it should be approached as self-critically as possible.' Along with sending pages to be read in advance, McLaren wrote a disclaimer at the start of her memoir, stating the subjective nature of her memories, and that she could not stand in for those who remembered the past differently. 'I think all families have secrets,' she says, and 'all have traumas, and many of them are buried. But what we do is we attempt in families that are close to create narratives we can all agree on so we can continue to be a family.' Memoir disrupts this. Speaking of family members, and their response to her memoir, McLaren says: 'They just wish I hadn't written it because they don't want to have to have a conversation about it, or to form an opinion. I understand that.'

You might think that writing about a family member who has died is the only solution. Legally and emotionally it does make it easier, but no less complicated. Benjamin spoke to me about how she would never have written about her father's sexuality or his violence towards her when he was still alive, but even after his death she felt reticent about exposing him. I feel similar, having written my memoir about my father after he had died. Interestingly Benjamin realised 'that reticence in me arose more out of a hangover of fear and a habit of self-silencing which remained with me even after he died – and which, of course, are the very things memoir is so good at confronting'. Benjamin, by questioning her reticence, engages with her 'noticing self', which is essential when double-checking our motivations. Despite this, Benjamin is not convinced that writing about someone who is dead is fair game as they can't defend their privacy or fight against potential libel cases, and I agree. What I struggled with, and still struggle with to be honest, even after publishing *Sins of My Father*, is that this is a version of my father he would not have wanted out there in the world for all to read. It speaks of me trying to make sense of the chaos of what his life became, but it also is my father's legacy. Only, it is a legacy written from my perspective, in my own words, and highly subjective.

Surely you would never write about your children?

Every memoir is different and demands that the writers ask different questions of themselves. A book about a cheating, lying father is going to have very different parameters from a book about the experience of being a mother. Because I was enthralled by my father, my voice drowned out in the greater, more chaotic needs of his damaged self, the act of writing about him was in part about finding my voice, about rising above his influence, and stepping out; whereas in a book about motherhood there would be no need for me to project my voice above that of my children. In fact, writing memoir and concretising memory and family experience go against a parental instinct to step aside and let your children find their own story, particularly at that tender time in their lives when they are discovering who they are.

Some people make a firm decision to not write about their children, while others justify writing about them because they too are part of the tapestry of life, and the memoirists' prerogative is to rise to a challenge. There are varied ways in which a writer might incorporate their children into a narrative, whether as generalised backing characters, as foils for the greater story, or as individualised beings, named and characterised. Is it possible to do it responsibly or sensitively? Or it is always too intrusive, and should be left well alone? Most important to me is whether it is damaging to imprint my view of the world on to one that is only just developing.

The first time I read Rachel Cusk's *Aftermath*, I was aghast at a scene where she describes her children crying in the bath soon after their parents' separation. 'Sometimes, in the bath, the children cry. Their nakedness, or the warm water, or the comfort of the old routine – something, anyway, dislodges their sticking-plaster emotions and shows the wound beneath.' Mine was a visceral response, as it reminded me of crying in the bath after my father left, probably at the same age as Cusk's children; I remember the pain, and it felt like heartbreak. I also felt Cusk's revealing of this vulnerable moment was an invasion on a private act of sadness and grief, which should remain in the safety of the family. I also wondered about the question of consent when children are so young.

When I first read *Aftermath*, I was still married, and I know that my reaction was in part due to my protectiveness towards my own children, but it was also a lack of empathy for what Cusk was going through. As I understood it, she had been the woman who had left, and a part of me was perhaps judgemental of that; now here she was exploiting her children for her own benefit. I was one of those women that Cusk writes about two pages later, whom she watches at the Christmas Carol service, insulated in their intact marriages, the safety of the nuclear family, two adults, two children, while Cusk, as a single parent, was relegated to the outside. (Maybe I was smug and didn't realise it.) But when I read this memoir again, years after a divorce, I underlined the sentences beneath this one about her children: 'It is my belief that I gave them that wound, so now I must take all the blame.' Because I too was feeling the depth of this guilt, I could recognise her wisdom, the wider reach of Cusk's critique, and her willingness to be tough on herself. She was a woman caught in the terrible contradiction of want and regret, evicted and displaced by a society that does not make it easy on single mothers. 'And for a while I am undone by this contradiction, by the difficulty of connecting the person who acted out of self-interest with the heartbroken mother who has succeeded her.' Cusk was writing for the divorced woman who has left, and I began to recognise also that her children featured only as an extension of herself. They are foils, a means of further emphasising this paradox, and the book would not have made sense without them.

I wonder also whether the question of consent only really comes into effect as our children grow more away from us. When they are babies and toddlers, they are still in many ways merged with their parents, and perhaps those same parents have a right to consent on their behalf. Consent, of course, has meaning for a teenager, whereas it doesn't for a child, who would not have the breadth of life experience to know what they were consenting to.

When my children were aged around 10 to 12, I stopped sharing photographs of them on social media, simply because they asked me to. Speaking with me about writing *Twelve Moons: A Year under a Shared Sky* and negotiating it with her children who feature in the memoir, Caro Giles told me she shared relevant sections with her oldest daughter, who is represented as The Mermaid in the book and was 15 at the time, but not the three younger ones. 'Even though I gave my children archetypal names on the page, to protect them, The Mermaid, The Whirlwind, The Caulbearer and the Littlest One, I had written very openly about her mental health and autism diagnosis, and needed her consent.'

Much of the outrage in the press against Julie Myerson around the publication of her memoir, *The Lost Child*, about her son's addiction to skunk and his eviction from the family home, highlighted his mother's betrayal – for depictions of her child as dishonest, violent and abusive – but also because of the question of consent. Myerson stated that her son had given her his consent to publish the book and to include some of his poems, but when he spoke to the *Evening Standard* to offer a counter-narrative around the time of the book's promotion, he said, 'I did see a copy of the book and I said, "is there any way to stop you publishing this?" and she said, "No.".' He also told the *Telegraph*, 'I was only seventeen, I was a confused teenager, I was too young really to know who I was or what was happening.' Teenagers are in the grip of discovering their own identity, moving towards their individuation away from family, and their parents' influence. It is a complicated time, as any parent of teenagers can attest to. But added to this was her son's addiction issues, which made him even more vulnerable.

When questioned about her motivation to write in detail about her children, Myerson said, 'I've always wanted to write things that feel brave. That make people slightly uncomfortable. I like reading work that makes me slightly uncomfortable. That's why I write. ... I need to be as honest as I possibly can.' But playing the honesty card doesn't wash. How can you be truly honest about someone else when writing from your own subjective view? You can be honest about your feelings and where their behaviour leaves you, but you can't give an honest view of their lives. Writing is too simplistic for that. The mother's opinion publicly expressed adds another layer of interpretation of a young person's actions, and therefore risks distorting their view of themselves. Tim Lott in the *Independent* highlighted the moral dilemma: 'she has got the balance wrong between the writer's desire to reveal the truth and the moral responsibility to protect others' rights to their truth'. What I take from this is that at that crucial stage in a person's development, let them tell their own story, and if they don't, and the need arises for you to share your view of that story, ask for their consent when they are an adult. Wait until they are old enough and clear-headed enough to know what they are consenting to.

My daughter is discovering her own way of exploring her subjective story, through her art, and there is nothing more satisfying than seeing this emerge at its own pace, on its own terms, as a form of delicate personal expression. I fear that, if I had published anything about her before she did this, my narrative might mould and bend hers, and it might take longer for her to find her own voice – as it took me longer to find my voice above that of my father's damaged self.

Try this:

1. Think of a tricky topic or part of your history you want to write about but are too frightened to tackle because of the ethical consequences.
2. Make notes of how you might enter into that topic either through metaphor, or the use of your imagination, or through research – focusing on the details around the experience rather than the experience itself.
3. Try writing about the 'ethically problematic happening', without mentioning the actual 'happening'.

My life, my life by Riley Dunn

My life, My life
Oh what a life
Delicious?,
Gracious
Oh what a life
The time wasted and the
time spent with good will.
Worth it?,
Spend it.
Oh what a life
The friends
The relations
The loved ones
The ach
Enjoyable ?
Exhilarated !
Oh what a life
The sex
The lust
The adorations
Infatuations
experience?,
emotional
Oh what a life,
My life, My life
Oh what a life
Sexy tasteful?
Juicy!
Oh what a life.
The ups and downs
The downs and ups
Oh what a life
Ice Cream?
Whipped Cream !
Oh what a life
My life my life ... in the sunshine

ACWG in 3!

Who gets the last word? Extracts from author conversations

You will have read the voices of various writers of memoir threaded throughout the text of *Into being*, but here I have collected some of my favourite quotations from the my conversations. One of the questions I asked writers is 'what do you love about memoir?' and many of them shared the memoirs that have given them inspiration, and also the feedback they have had from their readers of how their writing has helped give comfort, or change a perspective, or even change an aspect of their life. This can be the power of shared experience. I also want to highlight the importance of giving yourself permission to write, to call yourself a writer and to write about your life. The final quotations here I hope will help you find the strength to pick up your pen and to write through and beyond the stories that have defined you. You can read the entire interviews at lilydunn.co.uk

What do you love about memoir?

Noreen Masud: 'Memoir is probably my favourite genre. Older memoirs, especially. *Bad Blood* by Lorna Sage – that mesmerised me. But also the memoirs of early twentieth-century writers. *For Sylvia* by Valentine Ackland – I remember crying over that on a plane, in my very early twenties, as we dipped through sunny clouds ready to land in Edinburgh. Ackland was Sylvia Townsend Warner's lover; she was unfaithful and an alcoholic, and *For Sylvia* is an agonised reaching-out across that gulf between them. Memoir feels like a pleasure, where novels and poetry feel more like work, because of my job as a literature lecturer. I always want to know everything about people. Not what they did or wrote so much as what they liked to eat, how life felt to them, what frightened them. I think I feel so alien so much of the time that I'm always seeking comparison-points with other people's experiences of life – salt tastes salty to them too? Absurd, but there it is. I don't know what's ordinary about what I think or do, and what isn't, and memoir helps me think that through.

'When writing *A Flat Place*, I don't think I thought about how it would feel for the reader, except around things where I feared I might be misunderstood. I was committed to listening to those cries and whispers in my mind, and giving them form. With a flat landscape, and with Complex Post-Traumatic Stress Disorder, there are no ready-made paths to follow for talking about how it feels. All I had, as a resource, was what things felt like to me, in my mind and body – all I could do was to describe those feelings. So I suppose I wrote that way because no other option was available. Before the book was published, my main fear was that I would receive hate mail. I even wondered about whether my friends and family would be safe (and then of course I remembered that I am not important enough really to be targeted). I'd forgotten, I think, that people might actually like the book: that it might mean something to someone. And I've been stunned by the letters and emails and messages. One person said that it provided them with something to "feel continuous with". What a beautiful phrase. Another person – someone, like me, with Pakistani heritage – said she wished she'd had the book as a teenager. That was extraordinary. I wasn't ready for any of that.'

Lorelei Goulding: 'Ultimately, I think memoirs are full of hope; a memoir is often the tangible result of someone's effort to describe how they overcame something, and usually something very painful. I think writing a memoir is an act of artistic generosity too, because of the self-exposure that's required. But this is what also gives memoir its power, and its potential to uplift; the story is real and was lived. Someone survived something. I've relied heavily on memoirs as tools to navigate my own difficulties, and for me, memoirs that describe a harrowing upbringing – such as *This Boy's Life* by Tobias Wolff or *The Glass Castle* by Jeannette Walls, two of my favourites – always provided me great comfort that I wasn't alone. I guess this is an obvious answer and I wish I had a more literary answer, but for me, memoirs are my favourite genre because they are almost always about an overcoming, and I am a sucker for a story about real, human triumph.

'I think personal narrative is a potent storytelling tool; you know it is based on someone's actual experience, and this carries weight, at least it does for me as a reader, to know someone endured the thing they are writing about. I think where there is real power in personal narrative when the author explores a different aspect of the unspeakable, and gives the reader pause to consider something from a slightly different perspective which isn't focused on the spectacle of abuse or violence. Barry Lopez's *Sliver of Sky* comes to mind almost immediately; this wasn't just a narrative about the abuse the author suffered, or how he came to heal – it was an exploration about how that abuse affected his other relationships, and why his mother and stepfather may have made the choices they made, and the confusion it caused him during his life. Lopez gave us another perspective to consider, and opened up a different line of conversation.'

Susanna Crossman: 'I trained in theatre and art, and am inspired by artists like Charlotte Salomon, Louise Bourgeois and Tracey Emin who place the intimate and the prosaic on the canvas, the page. Memoir is inescapably part of this, making the personal universal. During the Yugoslavian Wars, playwright Sarah Kane found herself writing a rape scene and questioning the relevancy of her text in such a political climate. She comes to the conclusion that her rape scene is the seed and the war is the tree. This is also what the first philosophers were doing in antiquity, drawing lines between theory and the everyday.

'I am often drawn to forms of memoir/autofiction writing, but my life only interests me as material for approaching the human experience, exploring questions. It's like what Goethe called "delicate empiricism", a mixture of imagination, intuition and facts. As Constance Debré writes, "I believe in the human condition, which is something we don't know what it is, but it's being crossed by many emotions and hidden feelings, this thing that drives a path through us."'

Clare Best: 'I read a lot of memoir because I find people's life stories endlessly inspiring, moving, fascinating, almost as fascinating as the infinite number of different ways people find to tell those stories. I write memoir because my life (so far!) has been full of things that needed writing about. Writing the life stuff enables me to craft something particular (and I hope meaningful) out of it, and then move beyond it in some way ... But mostly I love memoir because it can be so many things – new directions and hybrid forms are exciting and innovative, and in my view very much at the forefront of what can be done with the art of writing.

'For the writer, there's a process of discovering and getting at that person's own truth, confronting it, exploring it, storying it, using all the craft aspects of writing that can be drawn on from every other area (not keen on the use of the word "genre" here) of writing.

'The transformation of lived experience into art is a magnificent thing, and it's in the space of the art that the connection with the reader can magically take place, in turn allowing for empathy and change in that reader. Influence and change on a grander scale can then gradually follow, in society – that's an exciting thought.

'Of course, fiction can change lives too, but in memoir I'd say the writer/reader connection can sometimes be more visceral because the reader comes to the writing with a sense that the writer really wants them to under-stand something vital from their own experience. So, the contract between reader and writer works subtly differently in memoir from how that contract works in fiction, I think ... And this: I've connected with many different individuals who've read the book, many of them survivors of child sexual abuse, many who had difficult childhoods and family experiences in other ways; some I knew already, others wrote to me out of the blue. I've connected with family in new ways. And all this has contributed to healing processes beyond my own.'

Pragya Agarwal: 'I like the idea of bridging the divide across a book's pages: for someone to read a story they might never have considered and see the rich diverse experiences in this world; or for people to see themselves in the pages of a memoir and not feel as ashamed or guilty of their own experience, not feel so alone. When we don't hear individual stories, it is easy to dehumanise people and stereotype them into one faceless mass. This is why these stories matter so much.

'Yes, memoir has the power to change lives. But this change could be a whisper of something that might not shift ground but merely transforms something in the internal state of the writer or the reader. And that seems more important to me. For a writer to be believed is a huge thing; for someone to read your life and believe in your testimony, when you might have doubted yourself your whole life, is such an amazing thing. ... As a reader, seeing yourself on the page can be so liberating. Since *(M)otherhood* was published I've had so many messages from so many people with whom my experiences resonated. One person left me a very tearful twenty-minute voicemail on Instagram because she was so utterly moved by it, and that made me very emotional. And that is just one example of many. I find the idea that someone would see themselves in my story and feel less alone or get inspired in some way, or change the way they live or think for the better, really moving. ... I also believe that real change can only happen from the stories of the oppressed and marginalised, so the more we are able to write – and read – the stories of our inner states, and of our marginalisation, those that have not been traditionally centred, the more we can disrupt these hierarchies in our society that push some people to the fringes.'

Vanessa Springora: 'In France, we have a long tradition of autobiographical literature. From Montaigne to Rousseau, right up to Proust, of course. I like novels, but I've always had a particular attraction to autobiographical accounts, the literature of reality, and what is now called in France "autofiction". One of my favourite books is the diary written by Marguerite Duras during the Occupation, entitled *La Douleur* [*The Pain*]. In it, she recounts her husband's return from the concentration camps, when she had fallen in love with another man. It's an extraordinary book. Not only does she record very intimate feelings from day to day, but she also bears witness to an era and to her activities as a member of the Resistance. With the desire to record an individual story like a self-historian, to keep a trace of it. Autobiographical accounts are often a literature of survival, and more authentic than the novel. Above all, it's about putting into words what is unspeakable. From a literary point of view, it's necessarily fascinating.

'I have often said that I don't believe much in the therapeutic power of literature. Let me explain. After my book was published, people often said to me: "So, you're feeling better now!" As if the simple fact of having made this story public was enough to erase the consequences on my life. It doesn't work that way. You need to have done some psychological work on yourself, or at least have some distance, to be able to touch others and make your own experience universal. What can really change your life and heal your wounds, however, is to see that your book is useful to others, that other people recognise themselves in it, and thank you for helping them to see more clearly in their own lives. That's so gratifying that it feels really good.'

Marina Benjamin: 'I love the way that memoir embraces contradiction and narrative disruption and personal discomfort, refusing to tie up all the ends. It throws all this stuff down and then demands you craft that irresolution into something possessing aesthetic integrity. For me, this fundamental difficulty is a large part of the air that memoir breathes. It shuns neatness and easy answers. It's also a very elastic form. Memoir lends itself to experiment in the same way that novels do, since there's no right way to tell a story. In some ways memoir is even more elastic because it doesn't need to be believable – and I think that novels do. Many memoirs strain credibility not because their content is outlandish but because people's behaviour is often extraordinary: irrational, self-damaging and/or violent, looping and insistent, dissembling or sublimating, etc. I'm also drawn to the way memoir allows the writer's consciousness to be naked on the page, for their puzzlement and curiosity and questions and troubles to become a driver of narrative. Readers want to be involved, to exercise their own curiosity and empathy, and it's easier for that to happen when a writer offers them a clear way in. By expressing doubt or puzzlement, asking questions and exposing your own dilemmas, you extend an invitation to the reader to join you in the pondering. Sometimes arriving at a good question is the point of memoir.'

Catherine Taylor: 'I have always read memoir, from Simone de Beauvoir when I was a teenager – in a kind of "show me how to live!" type way – but it is also a construction and an artifice, however authentic the voice or indeed the recollection. (I cite De Beauvoir because she certainly knew all about constructing a persona). It can change the life of the writer for good and bad – there aren't really any half-way measures. No word is ever the final word. Personally, it has led to some fascinating discussions with some of my closest friends about their own lives, and it has been brilliant to interact with readers more generally.'

Richard Beard: 'It's hard to make decisions and judgements without having all the information, that's the case personally, politically and publicly. And because there are connections and parallels between different people's lives, writing a book or painting a painting or doing any art at all really matters. *Omertà* is a word that comes up in relation to private schools, but it is true in private lives too. English reticence about being open about our private emotions, in particular. When we communicate, we realise we have much more to share than we previously thought and that can change the way people approach their daily lives and their relationships, the important things. To get rid of that *omertà* is important for the writer, but it can then lead the way for readers to do something similar.'

Anna Wilson: 'When I read excellent memoir, it doesn't matter about the differences between me and the writer – Alexandra Fuller's memoir *Don't Let's Go to the Dogs Tonight* tells of her childhood in 1970s Rhodesia and could not be further from the day-to-day of my own in 1970s Kent, but her relationships with her parents and siblings, her fears, hopes and the things that made her laugh resonate just as powerfully with me as though we were best friends from school. I think all good memoir does this; it connects us, just as excellent fiction can do.'

Jade Angeles Fitton: 'I read *H Is for Hawk* by Helen Macdonald and *The Outrun* by Amy Liptrot. And loved them both. *Lady Sings the Blues* by Billie Holiday is a masterpiece. A few others, such as *Featherhood* by Charlie Gilmour. I'd had a raven chick called Rookie that I'd nurtured, and so I connected with that. The more I read, the more I like the form. Most people have been through some kind of trauma, or lived through shame and humiliation, and they are such isolating feelings. You always think your experience is yours and yours alone and no one else will have gone through that, but I think the best memoirs are the ones that probably divulge a little bit too much, because that's what makes it feel real and how people connect to it. I was so nervous handing out the proofs of *Hermit* to booksellers. I went to Dogberry & Finch, a bookshop in Okehampton, and it turned out Kate, the owner, had already received a proof and had read it already, and she said, 'Everyone has a past'. I almost burst into tears.'

Caro Giles: 'I have used *Twelve Moons* as a campaigning tool to try to effect change for other parent-carers, which was not something I imagined would be an outcome of publishing the book. I have connected with so many readers – I get messages every week from people who have seen something in my story that has affected them in a positive way and this is the biggest joy of all. Such an enormous privilege. I wrote *Twelve Moons* partly to make my world bigger and that is exactly what has happened.'

Mary J. Oliver: 'In the last year, I've tuned into the true meaning and value of memoir. It was both sobering and inspiring to read Camille Kouchner, Rebecca Watson and Vanessa Springora, contemporary women writers prepared to describe, in unprecedented ways, trauma they'd experienced in childhood. And, even more significantly, the impact those events have had on the rest of their lives. The risks they took in exposing the tyranny of their abuser is heroic and a significant turning point in the refusal of women to be silenced. Transforming trauma and its aftermath into art and being heard at last, is a powerful tool with which to confront this scourge in society.'

Tom Lee: 'Writing a book can create a space of intimacy, a sense of people feeling like they've had a similar experience to you, or you've articulated something that they've felt. I had this with the essays I wrote (published in *Dublin Review*), but my memoir, *The Bullet*, will have a wider reach. And that feels like a powerful thing. I mean, that's got to be a good thing, I guess, to make people feel they can share something. I think we do maybe forget that what we've done is a bit out of the ordinary in terms of being so open. And people recognise that and it is a cue for them to be similarly open. After I wrote about my anxiety, a lot of people came out about their own anxiety, and it feels like a real privilege to be in that position as a writer, to help others speak out about their difficult experiences.'

Clover Stroud: 'One of the things that I love when I am writing is that a book triggers a conversation with other people. I love the idea that my words go into someone's head when they read my book, and if I meet them at an event or on social media and we share an interaction, then some of their experience will go into my head as well. There becomes a shared sense of humanity. I am a writer because I am really, really interested in human beings and the decisions that we make, why we do things, why we don't do things, you know, where we choose to live, where we choose to work, how we have been brought up, the relationships we choose, how they fail, how they work, our relationships with our kids, why we don't choose to have children, all of those things. I'm fascinated. And I absolutely love talking to individuals about their motivations. I don't know if this is catharsis. I think it's communication rather than catharsis.

'It's amazing when you feel that conversation is happening between people through a book. When *My Wild and Sleepless Nights* was published, I know it really helped a lot of mothers to feel less alone and less challenged by motherhood. It kind of legitimised what they were feeling and knowing that you are actually creating a positive emotional change and have helped people. And that's why, you know, doing events is really lovely when you get to meet people who come and say, your writing has really really helped me, and that's what enables me to keep on going back to the desk to write.'

Julia Bell: 'I am interested in reading witness accounts on how we live now, like Deborah Levy with her living autobiographies. Similar to Annie Ernaux. I love her work for the same reason. People say to me nothing interesting has happened to me, and I say, if you've got a curious mind, a short walk across a room is interesting. It becomes about the person who is looking, and the angle from which they look. Writers might write the first big book, which is the moment of processing the thing that they wanted to write about, and by doing this they also find their voice, their position, their point of view, like Melissa Febos did with *Whip Smart*. And now in her books we find that same point of view being deployed to tell the reader things about her life. So it's less personal, but the persona is more fixed perhaps. I think there is a process to go through to get to that point. The second book is more about your point of view – your persona.'

Damian Barr: 'Memoir is communal as a form. I was able to write my memoir because Janice Galloway wrote her memoir and Diana Athill wrote her memoir. We're all helping each other. You can't know who you've liberated and inspired. Every memoirist is chipping away at that edifice of silence and shame, we are all helping each other as writers and readers to do that.'

Jenn Ashworth: 'Memoir is kind of greedy and generous at the same time, right? And I do think that however painful or difficult the material is, the writer does need to be finally in a place where they want to put the reader first and offer something valuable. That's generous, but also kind of egotistical too, but all writing is paradoxical in that way.'

On giving yourself permission

Damian Barr: 'There is an expression I use when I teach. I call it self-privileging. It's the sense that nobody is ever going to give you a permission slip. The people in your life who have harmed you or those you have loved are not going to turn around and say "Yes please do write about your life". You have to accept it is a transgressive act and always potentially a selfish act, so you have to give yourself that permission. Some people find that easy because they are born with that permission but most people aren't and they have to work really hard for it.'

Pragya Agarwal: 'Writing our own stories takes a lot of courage. It is the combination of vulnerability and bravery in writing a memoir that really appeals to me. As the world feels heavy, sometimes all we have is our words. And when the world wants to silence our voices, writing our life stories feels like resistance. As a brown first-generation immigrant twice over, the idea of raising my head to say "my story matters", especially one that is about a woman's intimate bodily experiences which have historically been ignored in our society, felt like a bold move not just for me but for the women who came before me, and those following. *(M)otherhood* was not as much about the mind as about the body, and bodily desires and experiences have always been classed as inferior to those that are considered more cerebral. To write about something as mundane as mothering, giving birth, not having children, wanting children, could be labelled as self-indulgent. And I was aware of how ambivalence in women is not seen as attractive. I think we need to give more room to ambivalence. And so writing *(M)otherhood* felt like a rebellion, which was quite attractive to me.

'Sometimes writing memoir feels like lifting the lid on taboo, and bringing it into the open, giving it a name and a framework within which it sheds old skin and becomes easier to talk about. And sometimes writing memoir feels like letting festering wounds breathe and heal. But mostly it feels like owning your own story and finally being the narrator of your life. It is not often that we have an opportunity to do so.'

Susanna Crossman: 'The philosopher Paul Ricoeur writes about the importance of narrative as being fundamentally linked to memory and our perception of ourselves. Memoir can offer cohesion because the narrative/memory/experience becomes reframed as a story that has a beginning, middle and an end. We link together events that might be family secrets, or odd, uncanny things, the elephants in the room that have been ignored. It is a retelling and a telling. Also our role in a memoir is defined: we become a victim or a hero, a flawed, human character within a story. Finding the story we want to tell about a situation is the real challenge, I think. I've found the experience of writing *Home Is Where We Start* empowering, because I found a narrative shape and voice that felt right. I wanted to capture the mystery and beauty of my childhood, alongside the pain, and for thought to accompany feeling. I wanted to write about groups, architecture, homes and fashion, and the burning desire for change. It is empowering because it is a voice I chose, like a bespoke piece of clothing tailored to fit.'

Jade Angeles Fitton: 'Someone said to me, "You shouldn't write your story because it defines you." And to a certain extent that might be true, but I choose to view it in a more optimistic way. I might choose to write this part of my story now, but the next book will be different, and everyone's story continues to evolve. Writing is like the distillation of experience. If it were a stone, it would be quartz – the hardest most sparkling bits that are left after everything else is worn away. I tried to write about what it was to live through a particular experience. Soon, I hope to write about living through another experience, and then what is associated with me will expand.'

Marina Benjamin: 'I think one of the chief purposes of memoir writing is to confront the darkness inside of us all. I am personally deeply drawn towards the unspeakable and the ugly. I want to think and write about people (including myself) thinking ugly thoughts and behaving badly. Because it's only really interesting when people act against their best interests, or self-sabotage, or say one thing and do another, or strain another person's kindness or trust; or subvert agreed understandings or expectations. Or when they are driven by ego, or even more interestingly by id. Isn't this when our interest is piqued? I'm talking about ordinary everyday failures or character flaws as much as anything else, although I also think that family members do awful things to one another (behind the protective shield of the nuclear unit and the privacy that society affords it), and that sometimes these things are unspeakable. People frequently inflict themselves upon others or overstep boundaries in dreadful ways; they invade personal space, traduce the basic rights of an individual; this seems to me to constitute the unthinkable, not because we can't imagine such things but because we believe that it costs too much to tear down cultural and psychic institutions such as "the family". So we prop them up, against our own deeper knowledge of how things work – about which we pretend we know nothing.'

Julia Bell: 'I think memoir is a way of dealing with and packaging experience. It's not the last word, it's a version of experience and there will always be more to say than can be said in a small book. When I wrote *Hymnal*, I was trying to capture an essence, a feeling, an atmosphere.

It's not the last word on my childhood but it was very empowering to put it into words, have it live outside me, beyond me. I think of *Hymnal* like a song. Perhaps in the same spirit as Walt Whitman's 'Song of Myself' – poetry as an act of self-actualisation. The consolation of art.

'Ask yourself, why am I writing this story? What is the point of it? Maybe the sticking point is who is the person speaking or what is my time management? Sometimes writers tell everything in the first three paragraphs and then think they have run out of things to say. See if the events can be dug into more deeply than that. Take the reader into the moment and make them sit in that situation with you.'

Jenn Ashworth: 'There's a difference, I think, between whatever acts of self-care and therapy and coming to terms that a person might go through and how writing might belong to that, and what it is to write a book that offers something of value to someone else. Nobody really wants to read 8ok words of someone else's therapy, right? When I'm teaching this stuff, I try to let my students know it's super important that they look after themselves as they write the book – that it will be hard – and that sometimes looking after themselves will mean not writing the book. And that yes, they might expect to feel or think differently about the material once they're done – they should be prepared for change. But that in the end their final relationship with the reader needs to be generous.'

Clare Best: 'Writing *The Missing List* was the culmination of the process of discovering and confronting my past, and the beginning of being able to look into a different future. It's not exaggerating to say that creating this memoir marked a kind of slow-motion rebirth for me. I grew through the years of writing it, and I have grown again through the years since publication.'

Richard Beard: 'Part of the process of writing a memoir is that at some point the writer has to say I am a writer, I am setting this down on paper and I have a right to do that. I think you need to inhabit that state of being a writer in order to actually write it, as well as inhabit the experience you're writing about.'

Noreen Masud: 'You know when you're playing one of those old video games – where you can't save your progress at any old time, you have to reach a "save point", and if you die after that, that point's where you reappear? That's what writing *A Flat Place* has felt like. I have given form to – made concrete, in your phrase – something which was formless and chaotic; where I kept having to go back to the beginning as I thought it through, again and again. Nothing in the book was fleeting or forgotten for me. I was possessed by it all, every day, helpless with it. But writing *A Flat Place* – putting it in full, concrete, beginning-to-end form – has made a save point for me. I might progress beyond it. I might reach a different way of thinking about it. I might realise that everything I've written is wrong. Then I have the right to put it in another form. But for now, I have that "save point" locked in. I have a place to which I can return when my thinking about my life crumbles helplessly around me, and I can start from there.'

I am + have been with my
best Polly all day, she an amazing
feely in my tummy + I have
attention is to anything — the
more clear thought - something I
haven't even been much bright —
tell Lindsy he now? hope + what
could run that make think I do not
ete — crazy — but it is a feely
that I don't want to let go of
the anxiety

My fear is not and flach
not working — its the anxiety
has I fell — finally Xie is
me

Further reading

Memoirs written by authors interviewed

Agarwal, Pragya, *(M)otherhood: On the Choices of Being a Woman* (Canongate Books, 2021)

Angeles Fitton, Jade, *Hermit: A Memoir of Finding Freedom in a Wild Place* (Penguin, 2023)

Ashworth, Jenn, *Notes Made While Falling* (Goldsmiths Press, 2020)

Ashworth, Jenn, *The Parallel Path: Love, Grit and Walking the North* (Sceptre, 2025)

Atkin, Polly, *Some of Us Just Fall* (Sceptre, 2023)

Barr, Damian, *Maggie & Me* (Bloomsbury, 2013)

Beard, Richard, *The Day That Went Missing* (Harvill Secker, 2017)

Bell, Julia, *Hymnal* (Parthian Books, 2023)

Benjamin, Marina, *Middlepause: On Turning Fifty* (Scribe UK, 2016)

Benjamin, Marina, *Insomnia* (Scribe UK, 2018)

Benjamin, Marina, *A Little Give* (Scribe UK, 2023)

Best, Clare, *The Missing List* (Linen Press, 2018)

Crossman, Susanna, *Home Is Where We Start* (Fig Tree, 2024)

de Waal, Kit, *Without Warning and Only Sometimes* (Tinder Press, 2022)

Giles, Caro, *Twelve Moons: A Year under a Shared Sky* (HarperNorth, 2023)

Lee, Tom, *The Bullet* (Granta, 2024)

Masud, Noreen, *A Flat Place* (Hamish Hamilton, 2023)

McLaren, Leah, *Where You End and I Begin* (John Murray, 2022)

Millar, Ali, *The Last Days: A Memoir of Faith, Desire and Freedom* (Ebury, 2022)

Oliver, Mary J., *Jim Neat: The Case of Young Man Down on His Luck* (Seren, 2019)

Springora, Vanessa, *Consent: A Memoir of Stolen Adolescence* (HarperVia, 2021)

Stroud, Clover, *The Wild Other: A Memoir of Love, Adventure and How to Be Brave* (Hodder and Stoughton, 2019)

Stroud, Clover, *The Red of My Blood: A Death and Life Story* (Doubleday, 2022)
Stroud, Clover, *The Giant on the Skyline: On Home, Belonging and Learning to Let Go* (Doubleday, 2024)
Taylor, Catherine, *The Stirrings* (Weidenfeld & Nicolson, 2013)
Wilson, Anna, *A Place for Everything* (HQ, 2020)

Other memoir inspiration

Allende, Isabel, *Paula* (HarperCollins, 1995)
Brodak, Molly, *Bandit* (Icon Books, 2016)
Cumming, Laura, *On Chapel Sands: My Mother and Other Missing Persons* (Chatto and Windus, 2019)
Cusk, Rachel, *Aftermath: On Marriage and Separation* (Faber and Faber, 2012)
Doty, Mark, *Firebird* (HarperCollins, 1999)
Dunn, Lily, *Sins of My Father: A Daughter, a Cult, a Wild Unravelling* (Weidenfeld & Nicolson, 2022)
Febos, Melissa, *Whip Smart* (St Martin's Press, 2020)
Flynn, Nick, *Another Bullshit Night in Suck City* (W. W. Norton, 2004)
Gleeson, Sinéad, *Constellations* (Picador, 2019)
Guest, Tim, *My Life in Orange* (Granta, 2004)
Hsu, Hua, *Stay True* (Doubleday, 2022)
Jamison, Leslie, *Splinters: A Memoir* (Granta, 2024)
Leach, Cristín, *Negative Space* (Merrion Press, 2022)
Lenz, Lyz, *This American Ex-Wife: How I Ended My Marriage and Started My Life* (Crown, 2024)
Levy, Deborah, *The Cost of Living* (Hamish Hamilton, 2018)
Machado, Carmen Maria, *In the Dream House* (Serpent's Tail, 2020)
Murray, Tiffany, *My Family and Other Rock Stars* (Fleet, 2024)
Myerson, Julie, *The Lost Child* (Bloomsbury, 2009)
Ní Ghríofa, Doireann, *A Ghost in the Throat* (Tramp Press, 2021)
Shapiro, Dani, *Hourglass: Time, Memory, Marriage* (Alfred A. Knopf, 2017)

On the craft of memoir

Couser, G. Thomas, *Recovering Bodies: Illness, Disability and Life Writing* (University of Wisconsin Press, 1997)
de Bres, Helena, *Artful Truths: The Philosophy of Memoir* (University of Chicago Press, 2021)

DeSalvo, Louise, *Writing as a Way of Healing: How Telling Our Stories Transforms Our Lives* (Beacon Press: https://archive.org/details/writingaswayofheooooodesa/page/n5/mode/2up: 1999)

Gornick, Vivian, *The Situation and the Story: The Art of the Personal Narrative* (Farrar, Straus & Giroux, 2001)

Hunt, Celia, and Fiona Sampson, *Writing: Self and Reflexivity* (Palgrave, 2005)

Karr, Mary, *The Art of Memoir* (Harper Collins, 2016)

Lopate, Phillip, *To Show and to Tell: The Craft of Literary Nonfiction* (Free Press, 2013)

Singer, Margot, and Nicole Walker (eds), *Bending Genre: Essays on Creative Nonfiction* (Bloomsbury Academic, 2013)

Woolf, Virginia, *A Room of One's Own* (Macmillan Collector's Library, 2017)

Woolf, Virginia, *Moments of Being* (Harcourt, 1978)

Woolf, Virginia, *On Being Ill* (Paris Press, 2002)

On psychology, psychoanalysis and art

Aristotle, *Poetics*, trans. Malcolm Heath (Penguin Classics, 1996)

Bharata-muni, *Nāṭya Śāstra*, trans. Manomohan Ghosh, available at: www.wisdomlib.org/hinduism/book/the-natyashastra

Byron, Lord, *Don Juan* (Penguin Classics, 2004), canto III

Ferenczi, Sándor, *The Clinical Diary of Sándor Ferenczi* (Harvard University Press, 1932)

Frank, Arthur W., *The Wounded Storyteller: Body, Illness and Ethics* (University of Chicago Press, 1995)

Gilmore, Leigh, *The Limits of Autobiography: Trauma and Testimony* (Cornell University Press, 2023)

Hepworth, Barbara, *Barbara Hepworth: Writings and Conversations*, ed. Sophie Bowness (Tate Publishing, 2015)

Jung, C. G., *Memories, Dreams and Reflections* (Benediction Classics, 2010)

Kurtz, Arabella, and J. M. Coetzee, *The Good Story: Exchanges of Truth, Fiction and Psychotherapy* (Harvill Secker, 2015)

Ranganath, Charan, *Why We Remember: The Science of Memory and How It Shapes Us* (Faber and Faber, 2024)

Personal essays

Alnes, Jacqueline, 'What Remains', *Guernica*, 21 February 2019

Benjamin, Marina, 'More Primitive, More Sensual, More Obscene', *The Paris Review*, 20 January 2021

Further reading

Benjamin, Marina, 'Personal Growth', *Granta*, 11 March 2022

Billings Noble, Randon, 'The Heart as a Torn Muscle', *Brevity: A Journal of Concise Literary Nonfiction*, 8 January 2015

Cixous, Hélène, 'The Laugh of the Medusa', trans. Keith Cohen and Paula Cohen, *Signs: Journal of Women in Culture and Society*, vol. 1 no. 4 (1976)

de Botton, Alain, *A Therapeutic Journey: Lessons from the School of Life* (The School of Life, 2023)

Didion, Joan, 'On Keeping a Notebook', in *Slouching Towards Bethlehem* (Picador Modern Classics, 2017)

Didion, Joan, 'On Self Respect', in *Slouching Towards Bethlehem* (Picador Modern Classics, 2017)

Didion, Joan, 'Why I Write', *New York Times Book Review*, December 1976

Dunn, Lily, 'The Lost Children', *Aeon*, 7 January 2019

Hampl, Patricia, 'Memory and the Imagination', in *I Could Tell You Stories* (W. W. Norton, 2000)

Sanders, Scott Russell, 'Under the Influence', *Harpers Magazine*, November 1989

Strayed, Cheryl, 'The Love of My Life', *The Sun Magazine*, 2002

Walker, Alice, 'Beauty: When the Other Dancer Is the Self', in *In Search of Our Mothers' Gardens: Womanist Prose* (Houghton Mifflin Harcourt, 1983)

Woolf, Virginia, 'Sketches from the Past', *Moments of Being* (Harcourt, 1978)

Fiction

Beard, Richard, *Lazarus Is Dead* (Vintage, 2012)

Dunn, Lily, *Shadowing the Sun* (Portobello Books, 2009)

Woolf, Virginia, *To the Lighthouse* (Vintage Classics, 2016)

Film

Children of the Cult, dir. Alice McShane and Maroesja Perizonius (ITV, 2024)

Communekind (Child of the Commune), dir. Maroesja Perizonius (Lemming Film, 2004)

For Whom Do I Write? Robin Mukherjee, Tedx Wandsworth, available at: https://www.youtube.com/watch?v=26MjW-11208

Wild Wild Country, dir. Maclain Way and Chapman Way (Netflix, 2018)

Acknowledgements

This book evolved from my doctorate at Birkbeck University of London, and wouldn't have been possible without the support of Julia Bell and her belief in me. Also valuable were Richard Hamblyn's encouragement when I struggled with the critical component of my doctorate, and Jo Winning's guidance in medical humanities, which came at a crucial point for me to finally feel it was all possible.

Thank you also to my editor, Emma Brennan, who got in touch with me after seeing my Tweet where, in a fit of excitement, I scribbled about landing on something original and interesting, and she invited me to a meeting to tell her about it. With Emma I worked on a proposal and that is how *Into being* came into being. I am also grateful to Alun Richards and Rebecca Parkinson, and the team at Manchester University Press, and Daniel Benneworth-Grey for the lovely cover design. Special thanks to Marina Benjamin for our endless fascinating discussions about memoir, and also for being such a brilliant reader of my work.

Thank you also, as always, to my agent, Cathryn Summerhayes, and to Jess Molloy and Annabel White, for making up a brilliant team. And to all the writers I interviewed during the early stages of this book – your input was invaluable for giving my argument depth. I also want to thank my students for your enthusiasm, and unflinching loyalty. And the many talented memoirists I have mentored, who helped me formulate my thesis, particularly Carole Aubrée-Dumont, from whose process, and beautiful writing, I learned so much.

Thank you also to my mum, Jane, my brother, Ben, and my children, Dora and Arlo, for your tolerance of me writing memoir and all the exposure that entails! Thank you, always, to Robin for being my true inspiration.

Index

Index